How to Keep
Your Kids
on Your Team

Other Books by Charles Stanley

A Touch of His Power

Charles Stanley's Handbook of Christian Living

Enter His Gates

Eternal Security

Finding Peace

The Gift of Forgiveness

A Gift of Love

The Glorious Journey

How to Handle Adversity

How to Listen to God

In Touch with God

Into His Presence

On Holy Ground

Our Unmet Needs

The Power of the Cross

The Reason for My Hope

Seeking His Face

The Source of My Strength

Success God's Way

Walking Wisely

When Tragedy Strikes

Winning the War Within

The Wonderful Spirit-Filled Life

HOW TO KEEP
YOUR KIDS
ON YOUR TEAM

CHARLES STANLEY

OLIVER
NELSON
™

THOMAS NELSON PUBLISHERS®
Nashville

A Division of Thomas Nelson, Inc.
www.ThomasNelson.com

Published in Nashville, Tennessee, by Thomas Nelson, Inc.

Scripture quotations are from THE NEW KING JAMES VERSION.
Copyright © 1979, 1980, 1982, Thomas Nelson, Inc., Publishers.

Library of Congress Cataloging-in-Publication Data

Stanley, Charles F.
    How to keep your kids on your team / Charles Stanley.
        p. cm.
    ISBN 0-7852-6122-2
    1. Parent and child. 2. Parenting—Religious aspects. I. Title.
HQ755.85 .S73 2004
248.8'45—dc22   2003017877

Printed in the United States of America

03 04 05 06 07 PHX 9 8 7 6 5 4 3 2 1

To all the single parents who are working diligently to raise their children according to the principles of the Word of God.

CONTENTS

PART ONE

TO KEEP YOUR CHILDREN

ON YOUR TEAM,

YOU MUST **THINK** CORRECTLY

And do not be conformed to this world,
but be transformed by the renewing of your mind,
that you may prove what is that good
and acceptable and perfect will of God.

—ROMANS 12:2

ONE

VIEWING YOUR CHILDREN
AS GIFTS FROM GOD

⁓

THE SUICIDE NOTE READ, "MOM, I'M SORRY that I was ever born. It seems to me that I have ruined your happiness. I have chosen this way out so that you can be happy again." The young lady had been left with baby-sitters from the time she was born until she was old enough to take care of herself. At that time she was provided with a ride to and from school, an adequate allowance, and the freedom to do just about anything she pleased.

This young lady did not come out of a single-parent home where there was no option but leaving her alone. Her parents were simply too busy to be bothered. To spend time with her would have been an intrusion on the social commitments. Obviously, they had not considered her a gift from God. On the contrary, they viewed her as a hindrance to their lives and an interruption of their plans. And the parents conveyed this message to their daughter as she was growing up. They gave her all the material possessions she could ever want, but they never provided the warm, loving atmosphere for her that a child needs.

As Christians, we receive many blessings from the Lord, but of all the blessings, the most precious ones are those called "a heritage from the LORD" (Psalm 127:3). Other than receiving the gift of eternal life, the entrance of a child into the home is the most blessed event a young couple can experience. The children in your home are God's gifts to you, and He asks you to view them as such.

OUR SPECIAL GIFTS

Like many parents, Anna and I eagerly awaited the arrival of our first child. We both wanted children but decided to wait until we were out of seminary and into a church. After three years our desires were fulfilled; Andy was born.

When Andy was brought into the hospital room for the first time on the day he was born, Anna and I prayed over him. I remember as if it was yesterday thanking God for His grace in giving us a child. We thanked Him for the privilege of allowing us to have Andy in our home to teach and to guide in the ways of the Lord. At the close of our prayer we gave him back to God. We acknowledged and understood from the very beginning that although our children were gifts from God, they were not ours to keep. We know God had a plan for both Andy and Becky, our daughter.

We purposed in our hearts from the first day we brought each of our children home to raise them to know that God had a special assignment for them. It did not really matter to us where or what that would be; we only knew that they would be prepared by God with our assistance. Then we watched as God began to do His work.

AGAINST THE TIDE

In a society such as ours where children are oftentimes viewed as unwanted expenses and allowed to live only if they will not interfere with career goals and other such "important" matters, this principle sounds somewhat archaic. With the average number of abortions holding steady at under 1.5 million per year, it is clear that children are viewed by many parents as burdens rather than blessings. There is an undeniable correlation between the atheistic and humanistic trend in recent years and the shift in thinking concerning children. With personhood now defined in terms of quality of life, babies are not considered human until they demonstrate humanness.

This new definition of personhood and the ability doctors have to assess the physical and mental condition of the unborn have put man in the driver's seat concerning who will and will not be allowed to live. Once again man moved to usurp the authority of God. In doing so, another blow is levied against the foundational principles for successful family living.

It is not

what you think

that influences

your children,

it is what you

communicate.

Many children who have already been born have been called the unwanted generation. For various reasons the mother's pursuing a career seems more important than her staying at home with the youngsters, so the children are placed in day-care centers for others to raise. Linda Burnett, coauthor of the book *The Unwanted Generation,* says,

> I am certain that my children would not develop the confidence and security, on which they will depend throughout their lives, to the same extent at a day-care center that they would at home. There seldom is an adequate substitute for the real parent. . . . Raising a child in our day is both the most difficult and rewarding task God calls a woman to do. . . . The infant stages of our children's lives are brief and yet the most important both psychologically and sociologically. After they are little, we will never again have a comparable opportunity to shape the lives of our children for good.

This is certainly true since 85 percent of their personality traits are formed in the first five years of their lives.

Since *How to Keep Your Kids on Your Team* provides principles for how to keep a family together, we would do well to turn our attention away from the liberated left; their track record speaks for itself. In their inability to keep the family unit functioning successfully, they have deemed it an unnecessary part of society. In other words, they are abandoning the ship that brought them into and through this life, and they are leaving it to break up on the reef of their own creating.

Your decision to read this book is evidence that you are not ready to abandon ship. If you as a parent truly desire to keep your children on your team, you must begin by embracing the fact that children are gifts from God.

BOO-BOOS OR BLESSINGS

Some parents refer to the child of an unexpected pregnancy as a surprise or an accident. Such talk, however, reveals the parents' limited perspective and often leads to a subconscious grudge against the child. Worse than that, such talk, if overheard by the child, will make him or her feel like a mistake or an unwanted burden and can only contribute to the child's low sense of self-worth. So, please, if one of your children "surprised" you, let it be the best-kept secret in town. There are no surprises from God's point of view. Fortunately for us, God does not have accidents. What may appear to be a surprise to man is always within the sovereign plan of God.

As Christians, we must not use the same standards non-Christians use in determining the value and desirability of a child. The couple who has ruled out the idea of a sovereign Source is left to judge the value of a child according to the circumstances into which that child is born. However, present circumstances must not be used to determine the value of a child. *Children are gifts from God,* and it is in this light that their value should be measured. Anyone having doubts about this needs only to spend time with a couple who cannot have children. The psalmist could not have been any clearer on this point when he said,

Behold, children are a heritage from the LORD,
The fruit of the womb is a reward.
Like arrows in the hand of a warrior,
So are the children of one's youth.
Happy is the man who has his quiver full of them;
They shall not be ashamed,
But shall speak with their enemies in the gate.
                                        —*Psalm 127:3–5*

THE FIRST FAMILY

Eve's response after having Cain serves as a good illustration of this point. After she conceived and gave birth, Eve said, "I have gotten a man from the LORD" (Genesis 4:1). The Hebrew word translated "I have gotten" means "to acquire." This term combined with the name used here for God—YHWH (or One who can be relied upon)—indicates that Eve viewed Cain as fulfillment of God's earlier promise to her:

I will greatly multiply your sorrow and
      your conception;
In pain you shall bring forth children.
                                        —*Genesis 3:16*

She gratefully recognized God as the source of her first child.

Eve's response is especially interesting in that she knew the pain of childbearing was a direct result of her sin. Yet she did not associate the negative circumstances surrounding childbirth with the child himself. She saw beyond all that and recognized that Cain was a gift from the Lord.

BUT DO THE CHILDREN KNOW?

The question now arises, What kind of message are you sending to your children? If in fact they are gifts from God, do they know that? How do your children perceive themselves in the context of your life? Do they see themselves as burdens or blessings? How they answer this last question will pretty much determine whether or not you can keep them on your team.

I can remember as a child being the last one chosen when the guys were choosing sides to play basketball. I knew I was a burden to the team and had been chosen simply because I was the only one left. I knew that if I did not show up the next afternoon to play, no one would miss me.

You can imagine how low my enthusiasm level was as I took my place on the court. You can imagine how unmotivated I was to play. I was not an important part of the team; I did not feel like a part of the team at all.

To keep your children on your team, you must let them know that you wanted them to be a part of the team to begin with. The degree to which this is communicated will greatly affect their self-image and thus their ability and desire to function as a part of the family unit.

Jack Taylor says,

I find joy in receiving my children in prayer as gifts from God. As I do it almost daily I find that it enhances my appreciation of them and my fellowship with them. Matters of temporal importance become trivial before the eternal investment afforded of time with my children. As I take God's view of my children, I see them being formed into his image and receive it as a finished matter. I have seen the end from the middle and the matter is settled. (*One Home Under God* [Nashville: Broadman, 1973], 109)

Jack also suggests a prayer that parents might use in receiving their children as gifts from God:

Father, in Jesus' name, we receive our children. They are gifts from heaven to us. Forgive us for impatience with their immaturity. We receive them to give them back to you to be used to complete and perfect us that we in turn might be used to perfect them. They are what we need as parents. We receive them not as our eyes behold them, but as you intend to make them . . . perfect. We are delighted with your gifts to us and ask forgiveness for being less than completely pleased with them. They are to us a delight and a pleasure. We could not have made them more perfect than you have made them. We are happy to receive them here and now! In Jesus' name, Amen! (*One Home Under God*, 109)

Your children could be struggling with feelings of rejection because of some comments made in passing about the trouble their arrival caused you and your spouse in the early years of your marriage. Regardless of whether or not you really mean anything by these comments, you are communicating that the children are (or have been) burdens. Remember, *it is not what you think that influences your children; it is what you communicate.* What are you communicating to your children in regard to the role they play in your life? Do they view themselves as blessings or burdens?

As we conclude our discussion of this first principle, there are really two questions you need to keep in mind: (1) Do I view my children as gifts from God? (2) If so, do they know it? Incorporating this important principle into your thinking is the first step you can take in keeping your children on your team.

APPLYING PRINCIPLE ONE

1. Describe to each child the positive events surrounding his or her birth.

2. Remind your children that they were answers to prayer.

3. Relate the lessons God has taught you and your spouse as a result of the birth of your children.

4. If it was a problem pregnancy, make your child aware of the alternatives that were available but dismissed because of your desire for him or her.

5. If your child is adopted, tell your child about the prayers and the joy that accompanied his or her arrival into your home.

TWO

VIEWING YOUR CHILDREN
AS A STEWARDSHIP
FROM GOD

⟋

EDITH SCHAEFFER, THE WIFE OF THE LATE
Francis Schaeffer, answers the question, What is a family?
by stating that "it is a perpetual relay of truth!" She says,
"We as believers—who are in the Lord's family—are in a
race, each of us as an individual . . . with help given in the
race, from one to another, as we are placed in different com-
binations together" (*What Is a Family?* [Old Tappan, N.J.:
Revell, 1975], 119–20). She goes on to explain that many
have already finished the race, such as Jesus, who ran the
supreme race and the great "cloud of witnesses" mentioned

in Hebrews 12:1–2. Then she encourages us by reminding us that all the help we need for our race is found in the Scriptures. Finally, she concludes that this race is one in which God's truth is handed down from generation to generation, and the family has a primary role in this process.

The teachings in the Bible, of course, are very explicit about this. Moses said,

"Only take heed to yourself, and diligently keep yourself, lest you forget the things your eyes have seen, and lest they depart from your heart all the days of your life. And teach them to your children and your grandchildren, especially concerning the day you stood before the LORD your God in Horeb, when the LORD said to me, 'Gather the people to Me, and I will let them hear My words, that they may learn to fear Me all the days they live on the earth, and that they may teach their children.'"

—Deuteronomy 4:9–10

Another great message was conveyed from God through His servant Moses:

Hear, O Israel: The LORD our God, the LORD is one! You shall love the LORD your God with all your heart, with all your soul, and with all your strength. And these words, which I command you today shall be on your heart. You shall teach them diligently to your children, and shall talk of them when you sit in your house, when you walk by the way, when you lie down, and when you rise up.

—Deuteronomy 6:4–7

From the first chapter we learned that our children are very special gifts from God. Now we must come to understand that God has placed these little ones in our homes as a treasured trust. He intends for us to take care of them until they are mature and old enough to be directly responsible to Him. We are to see them as a stewardship from God, to whom we will be held accountable one day. Jesus said, "It would be better for him if a millstone were hung around his neck, and he were thrown into the sea, than that he should offend one of these little ones" (Luke 17:2).

Edith Schaeffer compares the family to a relay of truth. We as parents are to run the relay well so that our children and our grandchildren might know the true and living God we know and serve, and we are to see ourselves as stewards unto God for all He has entrusted into our keeping. We are responsible to Him.

AN ANCIENT ILLUSTRATION

Your role as steward over your children finds an exact parallel in ancient Roman law. In ancient Rome a child (particularly a male child) was under the control and care of a *tutor* until age fourteen. At that age a child was considered an adult. He was then placed under the care of a *curator* until he reached the age of twenty-five. (See F. F. Bruce, *Commentary on Galatians*, NIGTC, 192.)

The tutor and often the curator were chosen by the child's father. They had the responsibility of raising the child for the father, according to the father's wishes. They were to familiarize him with Roman culture, regardless of their own nationality. They were to teach him the trade the child's father had chosen for him, regardless of their preferences. These teachers were accountable in every area to the father of the child for the child's upbringing.

A Treasured Trust

In the same way, you as a parent have been given the assignment of raising one or more of God's precious creations. Certainly, you have a greater attachment to your own children than you would have to someone else's children, but the principle is the same. Your children are your *treasured trust* just as the Roman children were the treasured trust of the tutor and the curator.

Evidence for this comes from God's Word; He makes it very clear how we parents are supposed to raise our children. He has the right to tell us how to raise our children because in reality they are more His than ours. He created them, He sustains their lives moment by moment, He sent His Son to die for them and purchase them for Himself, and He is the One who has prepared for them an eternal dwelling place. They are ours for only a little while; they are His forever!

Being a Steward Takes Time

God has made it clear that we are to spend quality time with our children in order to teach them. The Bible says to talk about the things of God as we go about our daily routine, as we gather for mealtime, and as we take a walk.

The members of our family have learned a great deal while sitting together at the dinner table. We have found that the best time to teach our children something is when they are interested enough to ask questions. Parents, I encourage you to listen carefully to your kids, and when they ask questions, give them the best answers you can think of. If you do not know the answers, it is okay to say, "I don't know, but I will try to find out." By doing this, you not only tell your children you are listening, but you also tell them that they are important to you and they are worth listening to. In this way you are helping to build their sense of self-worth and their sense of really belonging to the family. These are very important things for children to know about themselves.

In his book *Positive Parenting,* Don H. Highlander says,

Learning never ends; it is a full-time job for both parents and children. The most effective method for teaching children is through positive family relationships. Clear communication, meaningful involvement and interaction, and caring relationships are the three keys to effective parenting.

As parents, we are working in partnership with God to bring our children from a self-centered lifestyle to a God-centered and other-centered basis for living. The failure to accept our responsibilities will lead to frustration, but step-by-step personal and spiritual growth will make us effective learners and teachers. And prayerful dependence upon God will give us inner resources beyond all we could imagine. God is always our model and source for becoming positive parents. (*Positive Parenting* [Waco, Tex.: Word, 1980], 165)

Ask God for wisdom in teaching your children His Word. He will guide you in more creative ways than you could ever imagine. A friend of ours is great at teaching her little five-year-old through songs, stories, pictures, and tapes. That child knows more about God than a lot of adults I know because her parents spend time with her, teaching her and answering her questions. One day she was quoting a new Bible verse for me that she had just learned: "Jesus Christ is the same yesterday, today, and forever" (Hebrews 13:8). I asked her if she knew what *forever* meant. Her mother looked at me and shook her head no. But the little girl spoke right up. "Yes, it means every day after today." We were all surprised. Her parents are certainly being good stewards in teaching her the Word.

AN OLD TESTAMENT ILLUSTRATION

There is no greater illustration in the Bible of this attitude than in the story of Hannah (see 1 Samuel 1–2). She clearly understood that her long-awaited son was both a gift and a stewardship. Her prayers indicate that she viewed God as the ultimate source of her son:

O LORD of hosts, if You will indeed look on the afflic-
tion of Your maidservant and remember me, and not
forget Your maidservant, but will give Your maidservant
a male child, then I will give him to the LORD all the days
of his life.

—*1 Samuel 1:11*

Her willingness to leave him in the temple to serve God
indicates that she understood her son to be a stewardship
from the Lord:

Now when she had weaned him, she took him up with
her, . . . and brought him to the house of the LORD in
Shiloh. And the child was young . . . and [they] brought
the child to Eli. And she said, "O my lord! As your soul
lives, my lord, I am the woman who stood by you here,
praying to the LORD. For this child I prayed, and the
LORD has granted me my petition which I asked of Him.
Therefore I also have lent him to the LORD; as long as he
lives he shall be lent to the LORD."

—*1 Samuel 1:24–28*

The text tells us that Samuel was taken to the temple
soon after he was weaned. A Jewish child was usually
nursed until the age of three. (See Eugene H. Merrill, "1
Samuel," *The Bible Knowledge Commentary,* [Wheaton,
Ill.: Victor Books, 1983], 434.) Imagine how difficult it
must have been for Hannah to give up her son at such a
young age. Hannah, however, understood that Samuel was

a gift from God, and she also understood that he ultimately belonged to God. As a result, when the time came, she was both willing and able—emotionally and physically—to let him go.

KNOTTED APRON STRINGS

One of the principles to be discussed later is the principle of letting go at the right time. Before parents can let go, they must understand, like Hannah did, that children are a stewardship; they belong to God. As long as you have the attitude that your children are "yours" and thus exclusively "your" responsibility, you will have a very difficult time letting them make decisions for themselves; you will have a very difficult time watching them make mistakes without jumping in to save them every time.

I can well remember the time when Anna, had to apply this principle and let go of Andy. He was sixteen years old and had just gotten his driver's license. One Sunday we had driven two cars to church because Andy was going to take some of the high-school kids to a youth function after the morning services. We have never needed many rules for our children, but one big rule was to *never* leave church during the invitation. That morning Anna saw Andy and his best buddy slip out very quietly during the invitational hymn.

As soon as the benediction was pronounced, I used to slip down the aisle to the back of the sanctuary to greet people as they were leaving. Anna felt that she would have to deal with Andy's infraction of the rule by herself since I was several hundred people away. When Andy sought her out in my study to get the car keys, she really felt that she should not allow him to use the car after all, since he had been disobedient. But, just as she was about to explain to him that he could not use the car, she sensed very strongly that the Holy Spirit was directing her to "let go of Andy. He is a young man now, and from now on his discipline must come from his father or Me. You will have a different relationship with Andy from now on. But you must not discipline him or seek to punish him ever again." She gave Andy the keys and told him to have a good time with the young people.

On the way home she told me what had happened. Andy was her firstborn child, and it seems that was the day she really let go to allow God to put the final touches to form him into the fine young man he is today. She had done her job well as a mother. She could still ask him to take out the trash, clean up his room, and perform various other chores he did as a responsible member of the family, but there would be no more discipline for misbehavior from her. That would be a task for me, his earthly father, and for God, his heavenly Father.

When you begin to realize that your kids are ultimately God's possessions and thus His responsibility, it will become increasingly easier to let them go when the right time comes and trust them to the care of their heavenly Father.

Nothing grieves me more than Christian parents who

discourage their children from going to the mission field or becoming active in full-time Christian service. They have raised the kids to be obedient to God, but when obedience conflicts with Mom and Dad's plans, it becomes evident whose ends were being served by such upbringing. Such conflict can be avoided if you as a parent will view your children as a stewardship from the Lord.

FATHER KNOWS BEST

Understanding this principle of stewardship will help you to let go and to hold on, too. Children are forever asking, "Why?" As their steward, you have the opportunity and responsibility to focus their attention on the ultimate authority behind all your decisions as a parent and an adult—on God as revealed through His Word.

As a steward, you no longer have to resort to saying, "Because I said so." You can explain to your children that you have been given the responsibility to raise them according to their heavenly Father's guidelines; you have found through the years that Father knows best. Explain that you have the responsibility to raise them in such a way that when the time comes, you can turn them over to their heavenly Father prepared to live successfully. These are not some arbitrary rules you have made up off the top of your head; these are God's guidelines that you are to follow in caring for your treasured trust.

If you begin to communicate this attitude to your children at a young age, they will gradually understand that though they are responsible to you as their earthly parent for a time, they are ultimately responsible to their heavenly Father. We will discuss this in more detail in a later chapter. Suffice it to say here that I believe a key to successful parenting is the ability to ingrain this sense of personal responsibility to God in the minds of children at an early age.

CONCLUSION

You must view your children as a stewardship from God. That is, they have been placed into your life by God so that you can raise them according to His principles to do His will when they are old enough to understand what that is. Such an attitude will give you opportunity to explain why you do some of the things you do as a parent. It will also help to develop in your children at a young age a sense of personal responsibility to God.

APPLYING PRINCIPLE TWO

1. Accept the fact that your children are a trust from God and that there is a sense in which you are raising them for Him and His purpose.

2. Commit to following His guidelines for raising children.

3. Explain the concept of stewardship to your children and how it relates to your relationship with them.

4. Explain to your children your responsibility to God as a parent.

5. Explain to your children how God's Word functions as the guideline by which you are to raise them.

PART TWO

And you, fathers,
do not provoke your children
to wrath . . .

—EPHESIANS 6:4A

THREE

DEMONSTRATING AN INTEREST IN THEIR CHILDHOOD EXPERIENCES

$\mathcal{S}$

ONE DAY A YOUNG MAN WHOSE WIFE AND children had just joined our church came to my office to talk to me. I assumed he had made the appointment to seek counseling from me. Instead, he had come as a Nathan to me. That is, he had come to take me to task. After we were seated, he looked straight into my eyes and asked, "Dr. Stanley, how much time did you spend with Andy last week?" (At the time Andy was around twelve years old.) No one in my family knew this young man, and he told me he had had no prompting from anyone but the Holy Spirit to encourage me to spend more time with my family, especially Andy.

I gave a lot of thought to his question for the rest of the day as I worked. I made a special effort to leave church a little earlier than my usual time of 6:30 or 7:00 P.M. I remembered Andy had mentioned several times that he wanted me to go fishing with him in a pond in back of our house. The pond was owned by another neighbor who had a rule that no children could fish there unless accompanied by a parent.

Andy loved to fish, and he and I had gone a few times to the pond to fish. They had been good times, but that day I was conscience-stricken to recall how long it had been since we had spent that much time together. Sometimes Andy would cry and complain to his mother about my not being there every time he wanted to go fishing.

I am so glad that God blessed Anna with wisdom in handling these complaints. It would have been easy for her to agree with Andy and complain about my absences when she wanted me there too. Instead, she explained to Andy on one occasion about my not having a father as I was growing up. (My dad died when I was seven months old.) Anna elaborated that if I had had a good daddy as a pattern to go by, I could have said as a kid, "Boy! I want to grow up and be just like my dad." Or if I had had a bad, mean daddy, I could have said, "Boy! I'll never be that way if I ever have any kids."

She concluded, "Andy, I think Dad is doing a pretty good job, especially since he had no pattern, good or bad, to go by, don't you?" Andy agreed with her and stated that he was glad he had a father even if his father couldn't always be there to do all the things he wanted to do.

One important aspect of viewing your children as a stewardship from God is demonstrating an interest in their future. Before this can take place, however, you must earn your right to be heard by demonstrating an interest in their daily, mundane, often trivial experiences. To keep your kids on your team, you must make a conscious effort to express this interest. In a past conference at our church, a minister said it this way, "Kids don't care what you think, until they think you care."

LET THEM IN

The family is the first group that children belong to. We always found it a good idea to let our children participate in some of our decision making, especially those things that included them. We called these sessions Family Powwows. We would discuss where we would go on our family vacation, what we would do for our Friday night family time, and other similar topics. I was always the chief, and we would "vote" on decisions.

The children always enjoyed these sessions. We would listen to their complaints and their requests. Many times our discussion might center on what kind of dog to get. Andy always wanted a German shepherd, but we felt that such a large dog would not fit into our family routine. Once Andy found a stray puppy someone had abandoned on our street. He brought the little white furry animal home and asked to keep it, so we agreed. That night Andy prayed that his little dog would grow up to be a German shepherd. The vet who gave the puppy its shots told Andy that it was not what he had prayed for but assured him that it was a nice dog. Andy was satisfied.

I mentioned our Friday family nights. These were usually outings such as playing miniature golf, visiting a special ice-cream shop, or occasionally seeing a movie. Sometimes we stayed at home and cooked outside and had a picnic. Or we would watch a TV program everyone agreed upon and eat big bowls of popcorn.

Since we lived in Florida during much of this time, we often rode bicycles in the evenings after dinner and sometimes at the beach. During this togetherness time, the children did a lot of talking, and Anna and I did a lot of listening. We were sharing some of our children's most important and formative years. I believe with all my heart if you give some quality time to your children when they are young, you are not likely to have the experience of difficult teenage years.

As a busy pastor, I did not always have as much time with my kids as I would have chosen, but I tried to give it all I had during the time we did have. I encourage parents who read this book to demonstrate sincere interest in their children and continue that interest as the children become adolescents and then adults. Even grown-up children appreciate knowing that their parents are concerned about how they are doing.

If you have a habit

of being attentive

and expressing interest,

your children

will not confuse

your loving instruction

with rejection.

A Tragic Illustration

A couple came into my office one afternoon to talk about their daughter. It seemed she had decided to get married against the wishes of her parents. Needless to say, they were very concerned and upset. They had done their best to get their daughter to cancel her plans, even to postpone them, but she was bound and determined to have her way. I agreed to talk to the young woman, and after some persuading, she agreed to talk to me.

Her story was one I have heard many times before. Dad and Mom were always too busy—too busy for the sixth-grade open house, too busy to see her cheer at football games, too busy for her pageants, too busy to meet her friends, too busy to help her choose a major, and on and on it went. But when it was time for her to choose a marriage partner, all of a sudden they had a surge of interest. All of a sudden they wanted to jump right into the middle of her life and help her make the "right" decision. All of a sudden her decisions were worth taking into consideration.

"Well, of course," you may say, "this is the most important decision of her life." That may be true, but when she was thirteen, the most important decision in her life was whether she should have her hair permed or leave it straight. But she was left to face that "crisis" alone. At fifteen the most important decision of her life was whether she should go to cheerleading camp or church camp. Nobody seemed too concerned about that one, either. Then there was the time she could not decide which dress to wear to the prom. Mom looked up from tossing a salad just long enough to tell her that it was her decision. Again, she felt abandoned to do the best she could alone.

For years an unspoken message had been coming through loud and clear: "As your parents, we are not really interested in what you do. It is your life, live it the best you can." So when Mom and Dad stepped in to stop the wedding, their daughter did not see their actions as an expression of love and concern. She saw their actions as interference.

Where Did We Go Wrong?

The mistake these parents made is a common one, one we are all prone to make from time to time. *They determined the value of their daughter's experiences and decisions while growing up by comparing them with the experiences and decisions of their own lives as adults.* As a result, there was always something more important going on; there was always a more pressing decision to be made.

These parents did not take time to view their daughter's experiences and decisions from within the context of her life; they never got her perspective on things. Consequently, they were unable to relate to her on the level she needed while she was growing up. As a result, a message of unconcern was reinforced again and again and again.

The real tragedy of this story is that these parents were genuinely interested in their daughter's future the whole time. However, their concern was never communicated because of their disinterest in her daily experiences. Remember, it is not what you *think* that will have an impact on your children, it is what you *communicate*.

To Listen or Not to Listen?

These parents made another common mistake in dealing with their daughter as a child. Not only did they neglect to consider her experiences from her point of view, but they related to her with the assumption that their personal interest in the *content* of their discussions with her determined their obligation to listen. In other words, if what their daughter talked about was not important to them, it was not important. Therefore, they felt no obligation to listen or show interest.

This was not a conscious assumption on the part of the parents. They never sat down and thought it out. They never decided as a couple that they would only listen to their daughter when they thought she had something important to say. Yet, that is exactly how they related to her as a child and as a young adult. The application of this subconscious assumption slowly alienated the daughter from her parents. When they suddenly seemed to take an interest in her life, it was too late; she was not convinced they were really on her team; she was not convinced they had her best interest at heart.

EARNING YOUR RIGHT
TO BE HEARD

Someday your children are going to be making what you would consider "big" decisions: where to go to college, who to room with, what to major in, whether or not to go to graduate school, which job to take, who to marry, and on and on. Your influence then will be determined to a great degree by your involvement now. You are in the process of setting a precedent with your children. You are either building credibility or destroying their confidence in you as an interested party. Again, your influence and involvement in helping your children make life's major decisions will be determined by your involvement now in life's mundane decisions. *You must earn your right to be heard.*

To express disinterest in what your children say or plan is to express disinterest in them as individuals. At least that is what you communicate to them. The important thing is not *what* you are talking about, but *who* you are talking to.

GETTING STARTED

You can begin today to express interest in the daily experiences of your children. To do so, however, you may need to change your thinking and behavior in some areas. You must gain a new perspective on your children's desire to share their lives with you. Imagine your son or daughter walking up to you and saying, "Mom (or Dad) will you be intimately involved in my life?" What would you say?

To put this principle into practice, you must realize that every time your children ask for advice or share the events of the day they are basically saying, "Will you be involved in my life? Will you be on my team?" This new perspective is necessary if you are going to express genuine interest in what your children have to say.

Another thing necessary in expressing interest is attentiveness. Look at your children when they talk to you.

Don't read the newspaper; don't fumble through the mail; don't stare out the window. Eye contact is in many ways more important than mental attentiveness. Why? Because *it is not what you think that has an impact on your children; it is what you communicate to them.*

I had a difficult time learning this lesson. When I was accused by my kids of not listening, I always reacted by trying to repeat back to them what they had just said to prove that I was listening. Then my son began to play behavior modification games with me in order to get me to be attentive. Every time I would look away he would immediately quit talking. This became rather humorous at times. He would be right in the middle of some highly emotional story and then suddenly stop as I reached for the mail.

Finally, it dawned on me that my eye contact was the greatest reassurance he had that I was really being attentive. The same is true for your children. Don't force your children to have to work for your attention because one day they will grow weary; one day they will quit working. When that day comes, your ability to influence your children will have been dealt a mortal blow.

A habit you might have to break is continually trying to change the subject. Again, I have been the number-one perpetrator of this domestic crime. I became aware of this in an unusual way. I noticed that every time my daughter would begin discussing something with me the rate of her speech would increase as well as her volume. She always seemed rushed. My response would be, "Slow down; relax." Finally, one afternoon we discussed "her" problem. Like my son, she had developed a gimmick to keep my attention.

She said she always felt as if I was getting ready to change the subject. As a result, she felt pressed to rush through whatever she had to say before the conversation moved in another direction. This is a bad habit for parents to fall into. It is our way of getting on with "more important" issues, but it is a guaranteed way to alienate our children.

A good habit to get into is to comment after your children have finished a story. Don't sit in silence. Ask them a question; tell them you are proud; laugh if it was supposed to be funny. The point is that you should express with your response that you were listening and interested. Don't be satisfied that you know in your heart you were listening; communicate to your children that you were.

But You Don't Know My Kids!

"But," you say, "you don't know my kids. They never shut up! If I don't do something, they will ruin every meal, every discussion, every potential moment of peace and quiet." You may be right, but that makes this principle that much more important. By giving them your undivided attention, when you have the opportunity, you earn their trust for those occasions when the subject does need to be changed, for those moments when they do need to be quiet, for those moments when you do need to glance through your phone messages.

Part of your responsibility as a parent is to teach your children when and when not to speak. But those lessons will be best learned in an environment where there is an overt spirit of interest and attentiveness on your part. If you have a habit of being attentive and expressing interest, your children will not confuse your loving instruction with rejection. They will grow up being able to discern the difference. However, where there is little or no attentiveness on the part of the parent, instruction will easily be confused with lack of interest.

As we conclude this chapter, let me ask you to think about this question: What was the topic of the last extended conversation you had with each of your children? To keep your children on your team, you must assure them from the beginning you are on theirs. To do so, you must express interest in the daily experiences of their lives as they choose to share them. Regardless of how unimportant their experiences may seem to you, remember that it is around these decisions that your children's world revolves.

APPLYING PRINCIPLE THREE

1. Initiate a conversation with your children on topics you know are of interest to them. Think of ones that usually tend to make you want to change the subject.

2. Get in the habit of maintaining eye contact during conversations with your children. Your spouse would probably appreciate this too!

3. Get in the habit of commenting on what your children have to say.

4. Quit making excuses for why you do not apply numbers two and three above.

5. Remember that it is not what you think that will have an impact on your children but what you communicate to them.

FOUR

LOVING AND ACCEPTING YOUR CHILDREN UNCONDITIONALLY

⁓

IN AN ACHIEVEMENT-ORIENTED SOCIETY SUCH as ours, there is a tendency to equate our significance or importance with our ability to perform certain tasks. Even as Christians we tend to evaluate our worth on the basis of what we have done rather than on the basis of who we are in Christ. As we mature in our faith, however, the Holy Spirit is constantly at work within us helping us realize where our true identity is really found:

Now we have received, not the spirit of the world, but

the Spirit who is from God, that we might know the
things that have been freely given to us by God.
—*1 Corinthians 2:12*

The tragedy is that when we put ourselves on a performance scale to measure our worth and significance, we tend
to put those around us on one as well. Thus, we accept others on the same erroneous and artificial basis that we accept
ourselves. Unfortunately, our children often bear the brunt of
our insecurity as adults. Our personal struggles with self-
esteem overflow in our expectations of them. Since we are
never quite satisfied with our own performance or looks or
whatever, we find it difficult to be satisfied with theirs, either.

The result is that we push and push and push. We expect
better grades, better batting averages, better manners, better
friends, better goals, and so on. Things are never as good as
they could be. So children grow up under pressure to
achieve a standard they find somewhat illusive and ever-
changing. They work to earn something that should be
freely given, that is, acceptance. And as one author puts it,
"Nothing can alienate a child quicker than having to work
for something that should be given freely" (Hugh Parham
Stanley, *The Challenge of Fatherhood in Today's World*
[St. Meinrad, Ind.: Abbey Press, 1982], 50).

Children in this situation tend to become workaholics
or to give up altogether and quit trying to measure up. In
both cases the parents have failed because the children have
come to believe on an emotional level that acceptability is
based upon ability to perform certain tasks or to look a certain way.

COVERT REJECTION

Unrealistic and ever-changing expectations are a form of rejection because you as a parent communicate that you are more concerned with your children's behavior as it reflects on you than you are with them as individuals. You may not think about it in those terms, but why else would you keep pushing them? Children may not recognize what has happened as rejection, but their deep feelings of alienation and hostility are characteristic of children who have been openly rejected.

FAMILY MEMBER OR EMPLOYEE?

Dad, I think we may struggle with this more than our wives. Our wives seem to have an easier time valuing and accepting our children for who they are instead of what they do. A woman seems to have an easier time looking into the eyes of her child and saying, "I accept you just because you are mine."

Time and time again I have seen this pattern in teenagers who come from families in which Dad is a professional of some kind. Doctors, lawyers, dentists, accountants, pastors, all these professions are exacting and performance oriented by their very nature. It is so easy for men in these careers to bring the expectations and value system of the office home with them. At the office, men and women are employed and promoted according to their ability to do their assigned tasks. The office is often a high-energy, high-productivity environment. Performance is the name of the game. Things run efficiently and on time. Employees who fail in any of these areas are considered less desirable than the ones who succeed and are usually treated accordingly.

The

development of

strong character

must be

emphasized

and rewarded

in the home.

After Dad spends eight or more hours in an environment like that, it is easy to understand why he may be somewhat performance oriented at home too. His expressions of love may seem to be related to how well he thinks his children meet his expectations. Dad may not actually say, "I'll love you more if you make good grades or if you mind your mother or if you do all your chores without being asked," but his actions may seem to reflect that feeling.

But even with all that working against you, Dad, you must change gears on your way home from work every day. Your children are not employees and were not given to you to be treated as such. They are to be accepted and loved on the basis of who they are, not what they have or do not have, not what they can or cannot do. This is the truth you must remember daily.

In his excellent book *How to Really Love Your Child,* Ross Campbell gives a definition of unconditional love that bears repeating:

> What is unconditional love? Unconditional love is loving a child *no matter what.* No matter what the child looks like. No matter what his assets, liabilities, handicaps. No matter what we expect him to be and most difficult, no matter how he acts. This does not mean, of course, that we always like his behavior. Unconditional love means we love the *child* even at times we may detest his behavior. (*How to Really Love Your Child* [New York: New American Library, 1982], 30)

STRIKING A BALANCE

"But," you say, "am I not to motivate my children to excellence? Am I not responsible to help them develop to the fullest of their potential? Are there not times when I need to push a little?"

Absolutely! In fact, motivating your children to excellence and improvement is in itself a part of expressing unconditional love and acceptance to them. To allow children simply to get by in life is another form of covert rejection. It is as if you are saying, "I don't care if you amount to anything in life."

If you are to motivate your children to excellence without expressing an attitude of conditional acceptance, two things must be true. First, all your prodding and motivating must be preceded by demonstrations of your unconditional love for your children. There must be *memorials,* so to speak, to their worthiness in your eyes. By memorials I mean events or conversations that have clearly expressed your love.

Memorials such as these are beneficial because they give you and your children something to recall for reassurance when you apply properly motivated pressure to perform and they provide a comfortable context for failure. Sometimes you will expect too much from your children, and they will fail. These reminders of your unconditional acceptance make it easier for them to face you when the bottom drops out.

Memorials can also take the form of a gift, such as jewelry, something related to a favorite hobby, a special item of clothing, or even the bestowal of certain privileges. In presenting the gift, stress several times that it is not connected with any particular occasion or activity on their part; you are giving it just because you love them.

The second thing that must be true if you are to properly motivate your children to excellence is that the standard by which you measure them must be their own ability, not somebody else's. In other words, they must be motivated on the basis of whether or not they are doing *their* best. Comparing one child's performance to that of another child eventually destroys the child's self-esteem, and along with self-esteem go expressions of individuality and creativity.

The real key here is to view each of your children as a unique individual. The assumption must be that each child is gifted in some particular area. Your goal as a parent is to recognize that area of strength and emphasize it as your child develops, for in these areas of strength lies your child's greatest potential for excellence. By cultivating these areas, you will do great things for you child's self-esteem as well.

Often your child's area of interest or strength will be something you are not familiar with or interested in. Do not make the mistake of downplaying an interest simply because it holds no natural attraction for you. For your child's sake, you must go the extra mile to become interested. But keep in mind that your interest must be genuine; a child can tell if you are not being sincere. My son is very gifted musically. Although I love music, I did not really appreciate the type of music he was interested in when he was a teenager. I wanted him to excel musically, but I must admit that I wanted him to excel according to my standards. Whenever I criticized his music, however, he understood me to be critical of him. Because children sometimes have a difficult time distinguishing between criticism of them and criticism of their actions or behavior, parents need to be especially careful to make sure that the message they convey is understood accurately. I'm fairly certain that if I had done this with Andy, our relationship would have been much more positive at the time.

There was a certain amount of conflict over this music issue that carried over into several other areas of our relationship. Looking back now, I can see that much of the conflict was totally unnecessary. The problem was that I was not as tolerant as I should have been as well as the fact that Andy misunderstood much of what I said about his music. Although in my heart I totally accepted Andy, my comments about his music communicated an entirely different message to him.

I am saddened whenever I recall that I missed an opportunity to motivate my son to excellence, in an area in which he was strong. The rift in our relationship was gradually healed as I gave up trying to make him fit into my categories and allowed him to function freely according to his own style and personality.

REBELLION OR CREATIVITY?

Along these same lines it is important for you as a parent to make a distinction between individuality, creativity, and rebellion. I have seen many cases in which a child's creativity and individuality has been misunderstood as rebellion. As parents, we sometimes have a tendency to fear new things when our children are involved. Our emotional involvement sometimes causes us to jump to conclusions that are not only wrong but also harmful to the self-image of our children. In attempt to "deliver" them from something we see as potentially harmful, we sometimes take away avenues through which they can legitimately express their God-given creativity. When parents do this, children usually interpret it as rejection.

One of the sweetest girls in our youth department became very interested in dance. She enrolled in some classes and began to advance rapidly. Her father had a very difficult time accepting her interest in dance. To him it was worldly, and he felt it would lead her into all sorts of undesirable things. When he finally approached her about it, a major argument ensued. He told her that she had a rebellious spirit and that her rebellion was the reason she was interested in dancing.

Nothing could have been further from the truth. She loved both her earthly father and her heavenly Father. Unfortunately, this misunderstanding led to other more serious problems until today this father and daughter hardly speak. Why? Because a parent went off the deep end and misjudged his daughter's interest in something in which he had no interest and about which he had strong convictions.

I am not saying that we should never give our children advice when we think they are getting involved in things that may be harmful. What I am saying is that when the time comes, we must bend over backward to communicate that we are not being critical of the persons involved. Sometimes this is extremely difficult to do.

YOU ARE WEARING THAT?

What children, especially teenagers, choose to wear can become a real area of conflict. Styles change rapidly, and every season seems to usher in something a little bit stranger than the year before that we find difficult to accept. Something inside us resists letting our children wear styles we do not particularly like. It is too easy to make little comments here and there to show our disapproval without coming right out and telling them to change. Most teenagers will take this personally, especially if we are not extra careful about how we say what we say.

It was easy for me to handle the clothes issue with my daughter, but with Andy it was different. I had a little phrase I used to say to him that I am ashamed to admit I used. When he would get all dressed up (to suit my taste), I would pat him on the back and say, "Now you look like my son." That was my way of saying, "I think you look sharp." But I was communicating conditional acceptance. We have talked about this since he has become an adult, and he admitted that when I said this to him, he wanted to respond, "And whose son do I look like the rest of the time?"

What I communicated in my remark was not what I was thinking. What I communicated was that I accepted my son based upon how he dressed. Do not make sly remarks about how your children dress. If something is inappropriate for an occasion, come right out and tell them; be specific. Don't say, "Are you going to wear *that?*" If your daughter gets ready to go out in something immodest, don't simply send her to her room to change. Sit her down and explain to her that it is because you love her so much that you think she ought to change.

Never criticize your children's clothes in public. That does nothing positive for your children. And besides, what can they do about it then but feel ashamed until they can get home and change? The best time to make critical comments about some article of clothing is after they have put on something else. This greatly minimizes the chances of their taking it personally and interpreting what you have said as personal rejection.

TESTING THE WATER

The following questions are designed to give you some indication about how you are doing in the area of accepting your children unconditionally. It would be a good idea to go over these questions alone and then compare your responses with those of your spouse.

1. How do you feel when your children make mistakes in public?

2. What is your initial verbal response to your children after public mistakes?

3. How do you respond to your peers who are aware of your children's mistakes?

4. Do you emphasize the development of particular abilities over the development of character?

5. When punishing or rewarding your children, do you clearly delineate between performance and value?

6. How would your children answer this question: What do you think it would take for you to make Mom and Dad proud of you?

EVALUATING THE RESULTS

If your children's behavior brings you personal embarrassment, that is an indication that your personal sense of security is being threatened. If your initial response to your children reflects your personal embarrassment at their actions, you are communicating conditional, works-oriented acceptance. Regardless of what you are thinking, that is what you are communicating.

A second thing that may be indicated is that you are overly concerned with behavior rather than character. Character is not something highly valued in this society. Our children will get little or no reinforcement for having strong character outside the home, so it is most important that the development of strong character be emphasized and rewarded in the home.

When children fail, parents have a good opportunity to demonstrate the difference between failing and being a failure. Learning to fail successfully is part of living successfully. (The principle of learning to fail successfully is discussed in more detail in Chapter 12.) Children who understand this basic fact of life will become better-adjusted adults than those who don't, and they will have an important element in their characters that will see them through many trying times. Parents must help children perceive themselves properly by instilling and strengthening positive feelings about themselves. When children fail, their response should be: "My performance is unacceptable," not "I am unacceptable." Parents who respond to the failure of their children by being overly concerned with their own wounded egos will miss valuable opportunities to help their children.

Imagine the following situation: Sue has practiced diligently for several weeks so that she will be prepared for her first solo in the school orchestra's spring concert. When her big moment comes, she misses her cue, and her whole performance falls apart. How should her parents respond as they drive her home that evening? Expressing how embarrassed they were as they sat in the audience will certainly not help her feel any better about herself. Besides, their embarrassment is nothing compared to the embarrassment she feels. Such an experience can be devastating to a child. Instead the parents should convey their love for her and offer their continued support of her. If she knows she can count on their unconditional acceptance of her—no matter what—she will be much more likely to develop and keep a positive view of herself.

AN INSIGHTFUL QUESTION

One good way to find out whether or not your children feel unconditional acceptance is simply to ask them: What do you think it would take for you to make Mom and Dad as proud of you as we could possibly be?

Evaluate the answer carefully. Is it task oriented? Is it performance oriented? Do they feel they must do all their chores every day? Do they feel they must make straight A's? Do they feel they must equal Dad or Mom in some business capacity? Do they feel they must make a team or a squad or perform some other public-oriented task?

Or is the answer more character oriented? Do they feel they would make you proud by simply doing the best they can at every task they undertake? Do they feel they would make you proud by obeying God, regardless of the cost? Do they feel they would make you proud if they were happily married? Do they feel they would make you proud by standing alone in a situation where they were asked to compromise?

The answer, if they are honest, will clue you in on what kind of value system they have picked up at home. The answer will give you insight into what you have communicated, regardless of what you may have been saying. It is this value system that will serve as a basis upon which they accept themselves and others.

Simply telling your children that you accept them unconditionally is not enough. If what you tell them is contradicted by how you treat them, you will fail to convince them of your unconditional acceptance, and you will cause confusion that could lead to more serious problems. Dr. Earl D. Wilson, a professor of clinical and counseling psychology at Western Conservative Baptist Seminary, says he has spent

> many hours trying to unravel the confusion that results
> from growing up with parents who *stated* one set of

values and *lived* another. . . . Living in such an environment results in confusion and sometimes even psychological maladjustment. (*You Try Being a Teenager* [Portland, Oreg.: Multnomah Press, 1982], 119)

The apostle John knew the importance of demonstrating unconditional love. In his first epistle he wrote, "My little children, let us not love in word or in tongue, but in deed and in truth" (1 John 3:18). That is my point exactly. Unconditional love and acceptance are communicated more clearly by what we do and how we do it than simply by what we say. When I need assurance that God really does love me and accept me unconditionally, I don't look for verses that say those words per se. My comfort comes from Christ's work on the cross. His death for me leaves no room for doubt, for He has loved us "in deed and in truth." In the same way, our children must have a backlog of memories to sustain their belief that we truly love and accept them unconditionally.

OBEY GOD AND DO YOUR BEST

When our children were growing up, we said two things to them over and over again: "Obey God" and "Always do your best." These two things served as the basis of what we considered excellence in our home. We never worried about how popular our kids were at school as much as we did about whether or not they obeyed God. At an early age, both children knew about the golden rule, the Ten Commandments, and other instructions from God. But we wanted them to do more than simply know about such admonitions; we wanted them to live according to what is set forth in God's Word. At every opportunity we reminded them of the importance of obeying God. Success was not determined by whether or not our son made the team at school. The question we asked him was, "Did you do your best?" Grades were never stressed in our home. The question was once again, "Did you do your best?" For our daughter, an A was her best in geometry; for our son, his best was a C. I highly recommend that parents adopt these two standards for raising their children because character development is clearly emphasized over performance.

GETTING BACK ON TRACK

As you have read this chapter, has the Holy Spirit made you aware of some ways in which you are demonstrating an attitude of conditional acceptance toward your children? If so, the following four suggestions may help you begin to turn things around in your home.

First, pray that God will give you insight into why you as a parent are so performance oriented in your own life. What is driving you on? It could be a simple matter of having adopted the world's definition of success. It could be an attitude you picked up from your own parents. It could stem from any number of insecurities that you have not recognized and dealt with. Whatever the case, ask God to give you insight into why you tend to measure your worth by your performance.

Second, focus on those passages of Scripture that deal with your relationship with Christ and the place your performance plays in that relationship. What you will find is that God's acceptance of you is based upon His Son's performance on the cross. Our performance does not earn us anything in God's eyes. (See Romans 5:1–2, 10–11; 1 Corinthians 6:19–20; Ephesians 2:4–10.)

Third, make a list of the character qualities you would like to see God develop in your children. Pray for your children along these lines. Emphasize these things in your conversations with them. Help them interpret their successes and failure in light of God's character-building plan for their lives. A good passage to have them memorize in this regard is James 1:2–4.

This last suggestion will be the most difficult but probably the most helpful. Sit down with your children and confess to them your struggle in this area and how it has affected your relationship with them. If God has given you some insight into why you are the way you are, share this as well. Point out your wrong assumptions concerning the relationship of acceptance and performance. Share with them how your career or your own upbringing has influenced your thinking in this area. Then share with them the biblical perspective, emphasizing the basis of God's acceptance of us as His children. End your time together by expressing to them how proud you are to have them as your children. Tell them you love them and accept them just because they are yours.

BEING A TRANSPARENT PARENT

There is only one thing that keeps us from being that transparent with our children, and that is the very same thing that perpetuates the problem to begin with—insecurity. *What will they think? What if they lose respect for me? What if they think I am being melodramatic?* are some thoughts that may be going through your mind.

Think of it this way. By making yourself vulnerable, you are giving your children a chance to demonstrate their unconditional acceptance. Do not worry about what they will think. In fact, this may be the first time you really find out what they are thinking! You need not worry about losing their respect. *Honesty breeds respect.*

Several years ago the Lord was working me over about some insecurities that I had been dragging around since childhood. As is often the case, these insecurities greatly influenced my ability to accept and love my family. As the Lord continued to give me insight into why I acted the way I did, I felt led to share these with Anna and our kids. A family vacation afforded me the uninterrupted time to share all that was on my heart.

We began talking at the breakfast table around 9:00 A.M. We sat there all morning, right through lunch, and on past dinnertime. We laughed, we cried, we hugged, and we all walked away with a brand-new understanding of why we related to one another the way we did. This experience was a turning point in my relationship with my whole family.

I share this in hopes that it will encourage some of you parents to ask God to give you insight into your own lives.

And after you have gained some insight, have the courage to be transparent and share what you have learned with your children.

To keep your children on your team, you must let them know the qualifications for membership. If it is a continually changing and unattainable standard of performance, they will either quit or live with the fear of being dropped from the team. If, however, they feel they are unconditionally accepted as members based upon their unchanging relationship with you, they will be more prone to stay on your team and function as a team member within the context of your family.

APPLYING PRINCIPLE FOUR

1. Ask God to give you insight into the standard of acceptance you communicate at home by answering the following questions:
   - How do you feel when your children make mistakes in public?
   - What is your initial verbal response to your children after public mistakes?
   - How do you respond to your peers who are aware of your children's mistakes?
   - Do you emphasize the development of particular abilities over the development of character?
   - When punishing or rewarding your children, do you clearly delineate between performance and value?
   - How would your children answer this question:

What do you think it would take for you to make Mom and Dad proud of you?

2. Ask your children the last question in number one above.

3. Pray for God to give you insight into your own insecurities.

4. Renew your mind to the truth of your unconditional acceptance in Christ by reading and thinking about Romans 5:1–2, 10–11; 1 Corinthians 6:19–20; Ephesians 2:4–10.

5. Make a list of the character qualities you would like to see developed in your children. Begin praying and encouraging accordingly.

6. Share with your children the insight God has given you concerning why you do the things you do.

FIVE

SETTING LOVING
LIMITATIONS

⁌

SEVERAL YEARS AGO ANNA AND I WERE asked to dinner by a couple in our church. After we were there for only a short while, all hopes for an enjoyable conversation were abandoned. It was like eating at a circus during the clown act. Kids were everywhere—or so it seemed. Actually, there were only two kids, but they generated enough activity and commotion for a dozen. Having raised two kids of my own, I know that children's emotions and adrenaline work overtime when company comes over, but their behavior was totally uncontrolled. We left that night with great concern for the future of those kids, for their parents had failed to set loving limitations for them.

When I speak of limitations, I am speaking of *rules*—the parameters of behavior for family members, what can and cannot take place. Without these limitations, chaos takes place within a family unit. When there are no clearly outlined rules, there is an endless stream of unmet expectations, and the result is frustration, which eventually expresses itself in anger and even violence.

RULES FOR RULES' SAKE

On the other hand, I am not advocating rules for rules' sake. That is setting up a bunch of do's and don'ts just for the sake of having rules. Parents need a planned approach toward setting up limitations. Decide what you are trying to accomplish by these rules; identify your objective.

I am afraid that the objective of many parents is to produce kids that always jump when Mom or Dad gives a command. Parents with that approach, however, often produce adults who cannot function outside an environment of clearly defined parameters; they destroy their children's ability to reason and think for themselves.

Let me share with you what I believe our objective as parents ought to be in setting up limitations: *We should strive to produce responsible adults who are able to function independently of parents' authority, yet wholly submitted to God's.* In other words, the system of limitations and discipline we set up in our homes should prepare our children for life outside our homes. If all goes well, they should become adults who live directly responsible to God within the limitations He has ordained.

WHY BOTHER?

There are two primary reasons for setting up limitations. First of all, *God expects it*. In Colossians 3:20 Paul said, "Children, obey your parents in all things, for this is well pleasing to the Lord." In Ephesians 6:1 he expressed basically the same idea when he wrote, "Children, obey your parents in the Lord, for this is right."

Writing under the guidance of the Holy Spirit, Paul assumed that the parents of these children had given them instructions. Whatever the instructions were, these children were expected to obey. Paul obviously expected parents to give their children guidelines by which to live, and he expected the children to abide by them.

I think it is safe to assume that God expects no less of us in the twenty-first century than He did of those first-century Christians. We are to set limitations for our children. This is a basic responsibility for parents. Not to do so is to disobey God.

You may be tempted to say, "What is all the fuss? All parents set up limitations for their children, don't they? The answer to that is a resounding no! Parents react to their children's unsatisfactory behavior in some fashion or another, but that is not what we are talking about. We are talking about a plan of action; a plan that has an objective; a plan that is both effective and flexible; a plan that will move children successfully from childhood to adulthood. Actually, very few parents take time to explain to their children exactly what they expect and why. That is why it is so important that we understand our responsibility before God to set loving limitations for our children.

Second, we should set up loving limitations for our children because *God models this approach to maturity development*. That is, God, our heavenly Father, has set up loving limitations for us. The implication is that limitations are necessary for successfully raising children. Both the Old Testament and the New Testament are full of limitations or guidelines for living. They are all-inclusive and clear. If we study these limitations as recorded in Scripture, four principles surface that are important for us to understand as we set up limitations for our own children. Let's look at each principle in detail.

DO WHAT?

The first principle is that God is clear; that is, there is no doubt about what He expects of His children. The best example of this is the Old Testament Law. Wow! Talk about precision. Here is one illustration:

> If a man is found lying with a woman married to a husband, then both of them shall die. . . . If a young woman who is a virgin is betrothed to a husband, and a man finds her in the city and lies with her, then you shall bring them both out to the gate of that city, and you

shall stone them to death . . . But if a man finds a betrothed young woman in the countryside, and the man forces her and lies with her, then only the man who lay with her shall die. But you shall do nothing to the young woman.

—Deuteronomy 22:22–26a

Suffice it to say that God is specific when He gives a command or sets a limitation. People were not always obedient, but they always knew when they were guilty.

In the New Testament we find the same things—clarity, specificity, preciseness. Paul wrote,

But fornication and all uncleanness or covetousness, let it not even be named among you, as is fitting for saints; neither filthiness, nor foolish talking, nor course jesting, which are not fitting, but rather giving of thanks.

—Ephesians 5:3–4

Here again there is no doubt about what God expects. It is painfully clear. And this is God's model for setting limitations.

Learning the Hard Way

Anna learned this the hard way with Andy. When he was thirteen, she gave him the job of cleaning out her flower garden, and that was about the extent of her instructions—clean it out. So he did. Boy, was it clean! All that was left was freshly raked soil. Not a speck of greenery could be found. No weeds, no onions, and, much to

We should strive

to produce

responsible adults

who are able to function

independently of

parents' authority,

yet wholly submitted

to God's.

Anna's dismay, no tulips, either. The problem was simply one of communication. What Anna expected was not clearly communicated to Andy. What resulted was family time around the trash pile as we tried to rescue the badly damaged tulips.

When you set limitations for your children, be clear. Tell them exactly what you expect and when you expect it. Don't say, "Be in early." Tell them what time to be in. Don't scold them for watching too much television; set a specific time limit. Otherwise they will feel guilty every time you catch them watching a show. If you do not want your daughter to wear a bikini, don't simply tell her to buy something conservative. Tell her you do not want her coming home with a bikini. Don't speak in vague generalities and then hit the ceiling when your children don't meet your unspoken expectations; be clear.

I can remember taking my son back to the barbershop several times after he had gone alone. Why? Because my instructions were, "Make sure you get a good haircut." After several incidents, it became obvious that our ideas of a good haircut were altogether different. I was not being specific enough.

I remember telling Andy to dress up for something and then getting mad because he was not dressed up enough to suit me. To me, dressing up meant a coat and a tie. To him, it meant nice jeans. Looking back, I can see that my lack of clarity caused many unnecessary confrontations.

God is clear when He sets limitations for His children. In following His example, we need to do the same. I talk to children all the time who feel pressured to live up to their parents' expectations, but they have no clue as to exactly what those expectations are. The results are frustration, a sense of unworthiness, and, ultimately, rebellion. Nobody wants to live in an atmosphere where expectations are undefined and punishment is quick. When we set limitations for our children, we need to be specific, clear, and consistent.

BUT WHY?

The second principle has to do with why certain limitations are given. In Scripture if there may be some question about why a certain thing is prohibited or commanded, God often moved the writer to include a reason.

Looking once again in the book of Deuteronomy, we find that God reminded the people of Israel of the limitations He set out for their forefathers. After a long and somewhat detailed description of how the camp was to be run and the limitations that were to be upheld there, He gave His reason:

> For the LORD your God walks in the midst of your camp, to deliver you and give your enemies over to you; therefore your camp shall be holy, that He may see no unclean thing among you, and turn away from you.
> —*Deuteronomy 23:14*

In the New Testament we find this same pattern of clear limitations with an explanation where one is necessary. In Romans 13:1a Paul set a limitation when he said, "Let every soul be subject to the governing authorities." That may sound a bit unreasonable today, but how much more unreasonable must it have sounded to the people in Paul's day who lived under the authority of a government that openly persecuted Christians? Knowing the confusion, he gave the reason for this limitation:

> For there is no authority except from God, and the authorities that exist are appointed by God. Therefore whoever resists the authority resists the ordinance of God.
> —*Romans 13:1b–2a*

Because I Said So!

I am afraid many of us are unfaithful to God and to our children when it comes to applying this principle. Many parents use the same explanation for every limitation they set down, "Because I said so!" This is both unfair and unhelpful. If anyone ever had a right to demand obedience on the basis of personal position, it was God. Yet He took the time to explain why He asked us to do certain things. If almighty God refused to pull rank when explaining limitations, who are we to dismiss our children's questions with a pious, "Because I said so"?

Such a response is usually the result of laziness, an unwillingness on the parents' part to admit a selfish motive in setting the limitation, or an inability on the parents' part to answer the question in the first place. All three demonstrate a flaw in the parents' understanding of the seriousness of parenting.

A consequence of failing to explain why something is

not allowed is that children grow up thinking there is no reason. If there is no reason, it follows that there is really no reason to obey, especially when Mom and Dad are no longer around to monitor behavior. That is certainly an unhealthy and undesirable attitude for children to carry with them into adulthood.

Children quite naturally make a connection between Mom and Dad's limitations and God's. Children may think, *If Mom and Dad have no explanation for prohibiting certain things, chances are that God does not, either.* If you don't believe it, ask your teenagers why they should save sex for marriage. A typical response will be, "Because the Bible says to." Then ask why the Bible says to wait. Chances are they will not know, and if they do, they will have to think about it for a minute. Is it any surprise that so many kids these days have stunted spiritual development?

As parents, we must make the effort to think through our reasons for setting certain limitations so that we can provide satisfactory explanations for our children. Our children need more to fall back on than a set of rules to obey because we "said so." To build their characters, we must give them principles to live by that have a solid foundation based on God's universal laws for successful living.

When Andy reached the first grade, he went through a stage of lying about almost everything. Unfortunately for him but fortunately for us, he was not very good at it; he got caught every time. We spanked him, but the lying persisted. Finally, I decided to try a different approach. One afternoon I picked him up from school and took him out for a strawberry milkshake. From there we went out to

Biscayne Bay, the stretch of water that separates Miami Beach from the city. We sat down on a park bench by the water, and I talked to Andy about lying. I explained that people who lie lose the trust of their family and friends. I told him the story of the boy who cried wolf. I did my best to explain on a first-grade level why God is against lying and why I did not want him to grow up to be a liar. That was all it took. Andy stopped lying.

When God gives us limitations, He usually includes an explanation. If we are to follow the pattern He has given us, we owe it to our kids to do the same.

OR ELSE!

A third principle in Scripture for setting up limitations has to do with the consequences of disobedience. God is clear not only about what He expects His children to do and why but also about what He will do if we don't obey!

Parents have a tendency, on the other hand, to be unclear about what punishment will entail. Do these comments sound familiar? "Don't come in until the grass is cut *or else!*" "If you don't clean up your room, *you'll be sorry!*" "If I catch you talking one more time, *you are going to get it!*"

In all the Bible never once was God unclear about the consequences of disobedience. It is true that some people were surprised when they were finally disciplined, but they should not have been. God always included with His limitations a clear description of the discipline that would ensue.

Going back to the book of Deuteronomy, we find this to

be true. After a detailed description of what was expected of the people of Israel, God moved Moses to include an equally detailed description of what would happen if they disobeyed. He began by saying,

> But it shall come to pass, if you do not obey the voice of the LORD your God, to observe carefully all His commandments and His statutes which I command you today, that all these curses will come upon you and overtake you.
>
> —*Deuteronomy 28:15*

Then he gave a full account of these curses, including the following:

> Cursed shall be your basket and your kneading bowl. Cursed shall be the fruit of your body and the produce of your land, the increase of your cattle and the offspring of your flocks. . . . The LORD will make the plague cling to you until He has consumed you. . . . The LORD will strike you with consumption, with fever, with inflammation, and with severe burning fever. . . . The LORD will cause you to be defeated before your enemies.
>
> —*Deuteronomy 28:17–25*

Turning to the New Testament, we find this principle to hold true there as well. In the New Testament the discipline of the Lord comes primarily by way of reaping what has been sown and losing rewards in heaven. For example, after explaining what God does and does not expect from believers, Paul warned of the consequences of disobedience:

> Do not be deceived, God is not mocked; for whatever a man sows, that he will also reap. For he who sows to his flesh will of the flesh reap corruption.
>
> —*Galatians 6:7–8a*

Then Paul warned of a loss of rewards when he said,

> For this you know, that no fornicator, unclean person, nor covetous man, who is an idolater, has any inheritance in the kingdom of Christ and God.
>
> —*Ephesians 5:5*

God clearly communicates the consequences of His children's disobedience. As parents, we are responsible to be equally clear with our children. Not only must we be clear in our communication, but we must be consistent in our follow-through. Anna learned this in a disciplinary session with our son.

A Soapy Lesson

When Andy was in the third grade, he began using a term that Anna decided was unacceptable. She scolded him over and over, but he persisted. Finally, she decided a specific course of action was required. She sat Andy down and said, "Next time I hear you say _____, I am going to wash your mouth out with soap." It did not occur to her until later, however, that she had no idea how to do such a thing.

She just prayed that the very thought of such a thing would keep Andy from using the word.

As fate would have it, however, Andy lost his cool one afternoon and out came the controversial word. Anna was in the kitchen at the time, and by her own admission she tried to pretend as if she had not heard him correctly. But she knew that to fulfill her responsibility to Andy she had to punish him for what he said, and she had to do it in the manner she promised.

As she marched him to the bathroom, still unsure of what to do, she spied his toothbrush by the sink. She picked it up, ran it across a bar of soap a couple of times, and then proceeded to brush his teeth with it. It was not a pleasant sight, but it was an effective lesson—one he has not forgotten to this day.

The point is this: Your children need to know what to expect when they disobey you. Even specific threats do no good if you do not follow through. Clarity and consistency go hand in hand when you discipline your children. Inconsistency because of your laziness or forgetfulness ultimately short-circuits the whole disciplinary process. With every limitation there must be a specific consequence to follow an inappropriate action. When this is the case, you will never leave your children guessing.

Include Your Children in the Decision

Many parents have found it helpful to allow children to have some input into how their disobedience should be handled. Let them decide the consequences of their actions. What you will find is that they will be much harder on themselves than you would be. Ask them what they think it will take for them to learn their lesson. I will never forget the time my daughter did something we all agreed deserved a switching. I sent her outside to find her own switch, and she came back in a few minutes later, crying. In her hand she had a stick about four inches long and about an inch in diameter. She said, "This is the smallest thing I could find." Needless to say, we found an alternative to her choice.

Match the Consequences to the Transgression

Discipline will be effective only if the consequences of disobedience are in proportion to what the children did. If the consequences are too strict, children may rebel even more. I counseled with a teenager whose father would restrict him from going anywhere on the weekends for weeks at a time for the smallest infractions of his father's rules. This young man told me that at the end of his restriction he felt like a wild horse just waiting for the gate to be swung open. He said, "When I finally get out, I want to go wild." Being too strict can create this type of attitude in children.

I have seen this same attitude in students who attend private schools where the academic pressure is more like that of a college than a junior high or high school. This pressure and the parents' insistence that the kids make A's result in a tremendous need to let off steam. Often children react by throwing wild parties, drag racing, or destroying property. Parents need to be sensitive to the energy of their children. If the form of discipline chosen tends to cause your children to build up nervous energy and hostility, you may be compounding the problem rather than solving it. You may need to reevaluate your decision on this point.

The other danger to look out for is not making your disciplinary action strong enough to be effective. The best way to judge this is to observe the effects of what you are doing. If no change takes place in the behavior of your children, the consequences you have chosen may not be strong enough to get their attention.

Concerning discipline, you need to remember the three C's. Be *clear* in communicating what you intend to do. Be *consistent* in your implementation. Be sure your disciplinary action *corresponds* to the transgression.

WHAT ABOUT THE GOOD GUYS?

This whole discussion of limitations has been somewhat negative to this point. Unfortunately, that is how we often present it to our children as well. However, the fourth principle our heavenly Father models for us in connection with limitations is a positive one; that is, He promises rewards for our faithfulness.

In Deuteronomy Moses preceded the elaborate system of curses with an equally elaborate system of blessings or rewards:

> Now it shall come to pass, if you diligently obey the voice of the LORD your God, to observe carefully all His commandments which I command you today, that the LORD your God will set you up high above all the

nations of the earth. And all these blessings shall come upon you and overtake you, because you obey the voice of the LORD your God.

—*Deuteronomy 28:1–2*

Then he listed the specific rewards of obedience:

Blessed shall you be in the city, and blessed shall you be in the country. Blessed shall be the fruit of your body, the produce of your ground and the increase of your herds, the increase of your cattle and the offspring of your flocks. . . . The LORD will cause your enemies who rise against you to be defeated before your face; they shall come out against you one way and flee before you seven ways.

—*Deuteronomy 28:3–7*

Here is a good example of the promise of rewards in the New Testament:

Blessed is the man who endures temptation; for when he has been approved, he will receive the crown of life which the LORD has promised to those who love Him.

—*James 1:12*

We usually do not consider receiving rewards to be a valid motivation for being obedient. God, however, has seen fit to hold them out in front of His children as incentives for faithfulness. In following His example, we need to set up a system of rewards for our children when they are obedient. That way the limitations we have set up will not be completely negative.

One good idea is to have some sort of merit system related to your children's chores. If they forget to do their chores, they should suffer the consequences; if they are faithful, they should be rewarded. If your daughter keeps her room clean for two weeks, take her shopping. If your son gets home on time every weekend for a month, pay for one of his dates. If your kids bring home good grades consistently over a pre-scribed period of time, extend their play time or television time. If they remember to take their plates into the kitchen after every meal, praise them and promise them a special treat, such as going out for ice cream or having a picnic in the yard.

Don't discipline them only when they are unfaithful; rewarding them when they are faithful is also a part of dis-cipline. God blesses obedience, and so should we.

OTHER HELPFUL HINTS

There are several other helpful hints to keep in mind when you set limitations. If you consider them along with the four principles we have just discussed, you will be able to more effectively attain your objective of helping your children become responsible adults.

Begin Early

First, *start early.* I think that you cannot begin too early to properly discipline your children. Of course, you must take into account the abilities and the level of comprehension of the various age groups. There are obvious differences between a six-year-old and a twelve-year-old. The important thing is to get them accustomed to living within limitations.

Unfortunately, some parents wait until their adolescent children get into serious trouble, and then they clamp down on the kids. If the young people have experienced little or no discipline in their early years, they will usually strike out in rebellion because they are unaccustomed to restraints. In the cases of teenage rebellion I have handled I have frequently found this to be the pattern.

Two Heads Are Better Than One

Second, *involve both parents in setting up the system.* A couple should always confer before either of them introduces a new rule to the family. Following this hint will eliminate a great deal of tension and confusion later on. For example, some children learn at an early age that their parents have different ideas about how to discipline. If one parent is more willing to grant privileges or is more lenient in disciplinary action, it is not difficult to guess which parent the children will turn to. This may pit parent against parent or parent against children, and the tension in the family will mount. Or the children may become confused because they never know quite what to expect. Remember that consistency is important. Such tension and confusion do not promote the smooth operation of the household.

Age Means Change

Third, *give increasing amounts of freedom and responsibility.* Your rules and limitations must be flexible. If your children are to become responsible adults who can function successfully outside your authority, it makes sense that certain limitations must be dropped or adjusted as they grow up. This does not mean you are compromising your convictions in any way. It simply means you are allowing them to decide some things for themselves. After growing up in your home, they should know how you feel about things. There comes a time, however, when they must be given the freedom to choose their own way, and it is better for them to be allowed to make those choices before they leave home.

Popularity or Principle?

When you set limitations, you set yourself up to be disliked. This is a real stumbling block for some parents. I meet parents all the time who are more concerned about what their children think of them than about what is the right thing to do. What they do not realize is that children who grow with little or no limitations will grow up despising their parents—the very thing that was to be avoided—because children interpret instructions as love and a lack of restrictions as rejection. An environment in which there is a sparse and poorly maintained system of rules produces insecurity and frustration in children.

If you are really concerned about your children's future, and you are really interested in keeping them on your team in the long run, you must abide by this fourth hint: *Never allow your fear of their rejection to be a factor in your decision making.* Saying no will always be difficult, but in the long run it may be the best thing to do. Not until we are older can we fully appreciate the wisdom with which our parents raised us. If you are faithful to what you believe is best for your children, they, too, will rise up and call you blessed in the years to come.

It Takes Time

Fifth, *remember that setting limitations takes time.* The time factor may be the primary reason many parents fail in this area. For far too many parents, disciplining their children takes a backseat to their careers, their clubs, and their recreational pursuits. It is done in their spare time, in between activities. There is rarely any recognition of the good the children do. Consequently, the children learn to misbehave to get the parents' attention. Setting up limitations and maintaining the system you have set up must be a priority if you want your family to function properly.

THE TASK AT HAND

This chapter may have seemed somewhat overwhelming to you. My purpose was not to complicate your life as much as it was to motivate you to discipline and reward your children with a particular objective in mind. God's grace is more than sufficient when you forget or go overboard, so don't panic. But please take some time to evaluate how you go about setting up the system of rules and limitations in your home. Review the principles God has modeled in His relationship with us, and then ask Him to give you wisdom as you seek to establish a system in your home that will serve as another step toward keeping your kids on your team.

APPLYING PRINCIPLE FIVE

1. Establish an objective for your system of rules. What are you hoping to accomplish?

2. Make your rules clear. Ask your children to repeat them back to you to see if they really understand.

3. Explain the principle behind each rule; in other words, explain why the rule is there to begin with.

4. Attach some disciplinary action to each rule or set of rules.

5. Make sure the consequence corresponds to the transgression.

6. Be consistent in carrying out disciplinary action.

7. Develop a system of rewards for consistent obedience.

8. Begin early in your children's lives.

9. Increase responsibility and freedom with the age of the children.

10. Be willing to be unpopular for a while.

11. Take time to follow through.

PART THREE

To keep your children

on your team,

you must TEACH them correctly

...*but bring them up
in the training and admonition
of the Lord.*

—EPHESIANS 6:4B

SIX

HANDING DOWN
YOUR FAITH

♆

HAVE YOU EVER THOUGHT ABOUT WHAT YOU
are going to leave behind when you die? Most people think in
terms of possessions—property, money, stocks and bonds, and
so forth. But let's think in terms of what kind of faith you are
going to leave your children. What kind of spiritual heritage,
what kind of lifestyle, what kind of understanding of who God
is and of what the Scriptures say will be your legacy?

BEGIN NOW

You may say, "Wait a minute. You can't give someone else
your faith. That is something everyone has to experience on

a personal basis. You can't really give your faith away." You cannot give away your experience, I admit, but you can hand down your faith. You can leave your sense of moral values, your understanding of the principles of Scripture, those principles of the Word of God that have guided you and led you as you made your decisions in life.

Actually, you should begin to hand down your faith to your children now while they are still young and in your home. When you pray with them, discipline them, play games with them or read to them, help a neighbor in distress, or treat your spouse with respect you illustrate your understanding of God's commands. But their acceptance of what you are trying to hand down is another matter.

I am sure you know of children whose parents are active church members or even Christian leaders, yet they grow up and depart from the faith of their parents. They may absolutely rebel against the Christian lifestyle of their parents. How can that be explained?

There are probably several reasons, but the primary one is that many Christian parents, parents who really love God, do not know how to pass on their spiritual heritage to their children. Parents cannot cram faith down the throats of their children or force it upon them. Parents cannot *make* children believe what they believe. What do you think will happen if parents say, "Here is our doctrine, and we want you to believe what we believe. If it is good enough for us, it is good enough for you"? Children do not accept that approach, and I do not really blame them. They need more explanation than that to build into them a real understanding of why they believe what they believe. And it may be that what is good for the parents is not necessarily good for the children.

The greatest

motivation

in the world

for learning

is praise.

A New Testament Success Story

"Well," you may ask, "is there a way of handing down my faith which my children will find acceptable?" Yes, there is a way, and the apostle Paul wrote about what can happen when faith is successfully handed down. Young Timothy was a minister, and Paul addressed these words to him:

> Paul, an apostle of Jesus Christ by the will of God, according to the promise of life which is in Christ Jesus, to Timothy, a beloved son: Grace, mercy, and peace from God the Father and Christ Jesus our Lord. I thank God, whom I serve with a pure conscience, as my forefathers did, as without ceasing I remember you in my prayers night and day, greatly desiring to see you, being mindful of your tears, that I may be filled with joy, when I call to remembrance the genuine faith that is in you, which dwelt first in your grandmother Lois and your mother Eunice, and I am persuaded is in you also. Therefore I remind you to stir up the gift of God which is in you through the laying on of my hands. For God has not given us a spirit of fear, but of power and of love and of a sound mind.
>
> —*2 Timothy 1:1–7*

Let me give you a little background about Timothy before we go any further. He was born of a pagan Greek father and a very devout Jewish mother. The Scriptures tell us that he was an admirable young man who was converted during Paul's first missionary journey. Paul chose him to be a companion on his second missionary journey, and he left the young man in different areas to serve as pastor to the people who had been won to Christ.

When Paul wrote the two epistles bearing Timothy's name, the young man was going through a trying time in the pastorate, and he was about to lose heart. His faith was beginning to weaken, so Paul wrote him to boost his faith. In effect, Paul was saying in the verses included here, "Timothy, I remember the faith of your grandmother and the faith of your mother, and I am persuaded that the same quality of sincere faith is in you. I saw that in you when I chose you as a partner in my missionary work. At this point in your life when you may be a little discouraged in your ministry, you are to rekindle the flame that I know is within you. Put the bellows to work to blow against those coals that are just smoldering. Keep using the bellows until those smoldering coals become red and then white with heat, until they flame up once again unto the fervor and the commitment and the excitement that you have for the Lord Jesus Christ in the ministry to which he has called you."

Paul knew that this young man had a genuine, sincere faith as a strong foundation for his life. It was the faith that Paul witnessed in Timothy's grandmother and mother and in Timothy himself. And Paul knew that he had built upon this foundation to equip Timothy to be a tremendously effective servant of the Lord.

You Have to Have Faith

How did the two women, Lois and Eunice, so equip young Timothy that Paul could say, "There is a prize for God. I am going to invest my life in this young man. I am going to take him with me on my missionary journey. He has absolutely tremendous potential to serve the living God"? What grandmother and mother would not like the privilege of being able to hand down such a faith so that God one day would choose the grandchildren and the children to be used of Him mightily in His service somewhere in the world? Who would not want to be able to hand down a faith that would equip children to be successful as servants of the living God? The truth is that you cannot hand down something you do not have. I do not know exactly what steps this grandmother and this mother took to hand down their faith, but it is clear that they had a heritage to pass on.

What about you? How do you answer the question, At this moment in your life, do you have a faith to leave your children? Are there principles, guiding spiritual, biblical principles, in your life that have become a vital part of your thinking and living? As a believer, have you ever thought about some of the spiritual principles that God has taught you? Are you willing to sit down and write out what you want your children to remember?

I encourage you now to take the time to write out the principles, the spiritual truths, that have worked in your life. What principles have you exercised that have caused God to prosper you in return? You must have an idea of what you want your children to remember before you can pass it on to them, and this list will help you clarify these points. Keep this list beside you as you read the rest of this chapter. You may want to add some things to it or make notes about some points we will discuss.

Six Words

When our children were still small, I tried to figure out how to go about handing down my faith to them. After a lot of thought and prayer, I summarized my approach in six words. As we discuss each one, I encourage you to think of ways you may apply these ideas in the life of your family. Jot down your ideas and begin practicing them gradually, one at a time.

Principle

First of all, we hand down our faith by *principle*. By that I mean instructing our children in the ways of God.

An important passage in the book of Deuteronomy speaks directly to this subject. When the children of Israel came out of Egyptian bondage, God spoke to Moses and told him to prepare the people for entering the Promised Land. He knew that they were going in among a heathen people and that they would be tempted to forget the God who brought them out of Egypt and across the Red Sea. And as generations passed, it would be very easy for them to forget what their parents had experienced. So He had Moses give some strong words of admonition to the people of Israel to pass on to their children:

> Hear, O Israel: The LORD our God, the LORD is one! You shall love the LORD your God with all your heart, with all your soul, and with all your strength. And these words which I command you today shall be in your heart.
>
> —*Deuteronomy 6:4–6*

Note that Moses said "in your heart." That is, you are to become emotional about these truths. They are so precious, so profound, so absolutely essential to God's purpose in your life that they are to be upon your heart.

Then he said, "You shall teach them diligently to your children" (Deuteronomy 6:7a). You are to teach them *diligently*. You are to be willing to invest the time, the effort, and the energy to teach your children these truths.

Moses continued,

And [you] shall talk of them when you sit in your house, when you walk by the way, when you lie down, and when you rise up.

—*Deuteronomy 6:7b*

Your whole life is to be absolutely permeated and saturated by the teachings of the Word of God. As you go about your daily routine and your work, these principles will direct your thought patterns and govern your actions. These principles of Scripture will color your whole perspective on the experiences of your life.

Moses went a step further:

You shall bind them as a sign on your hand, and they shall be as frontlets between your eyes. You shall write them on the doorposts of your house and on your gates.

—*Deuteronomy 6:8–9*

And that is just what they did. These principles were so important that they put them in little boxes and strapped them to their foreheads and to their wrists. They wrote them on the doorposts of their homes and put them in small boxes on the doorposts. They surrounded themselves with reminders of God's principles.

How do we hand down our faith? By instructing our children in the Word of God.

I would like you to honestly answer some questions. According to the Word of God, mothers and fathers (but primarily fathers) have the responsibility of instructing children in the things of God. But when was the last time you took the Word of God and sat down with your children to explain a passage of Scripture? When was the last time you explained some spiritual principle that you learned in a Sunday morning or evening worship service? When was the last time your children brought up an issue, and you referred to a biblical passage because God said something specific about it?

This is not an option. This is a command of God that we are to instruct our children in the ways of God and pass on our faith. That is what God was saying to Moses and the people of Israel.

What is the schedule in your home each evening? (Or is schedule the wrong word to describe what happens?) Do the members of your family get together for the evening meal, bolt their food, and dash off to watch something on television, never to move again until bedtime? Or do the members or your family sit down to eat, talk about a lot of different subjects and share experiences of the day, and maybe spend some time together after the dishes?

How many spiritual principles can children learn on any given evening by watching television? I am talking about all kinds of programs—funny ones, good ones, bad ones, you name it. Even in the far-above-average American family that calls itself Christian, many parents spend time watching television with their children but give no time to instructing them about how to live based on the principles of Scripture.

You do not have to bring out the big, black, four-inch-thick family Bible, set it on the dining table, and say, "We are going to study the principles of the Bible." That approach would probably do more harm than good. Just take advantage of the opportunity while sitting around the table to weave the Word of God into your conversation about whatever subject happens to surface. Follow the advice of Scripture to talk of the things of God when you are seated, when you stand, when you walk, when you arise, and when you lie down.

I can remember reading Bible stories to our children. Some nights I would go in, read a story, and my mind would wander into all the things I had to do after I finished the story. About the time I would finish, Andy would say, "Read it again, Dad. Just one more time." And I would read it again, and we would talk about the story. I have read the same story several times in one night. I have never regretted doing that, and our children still remember our times together. These precious times were important periods of learning for my children.

I do not know what television programs you watch on any given evening, but whatever they are, they are not nearly as important as spending time with your children and talking about the things of God. Share your experiences and your feelings so that your children can learn from them.

You may protest, "I just don't know how to start."

Here is the way to start. Find out what your children are interested in, and then talk about those things and weave the truths of God into what you discuss. That is the way to hand down your faith.

Do not give your children twenty-five verses of Scripture to memorize by tomorrow night. Rote memorization is not what you are trying to accomplish. Any parent can say, "Memory verse for tomorrow night is 1 John 1:9," and the parent may not even know it. The best approach is to weave the meaning of that verse into your conversation and show how it applies in real-life situations. Children must know what the verses mean to you if they are to learn about their faith, about what you believe, why you believe it, and how it all works in your life.

Pattern

Second, we hand down our faith by *pattern*. Children probably learn more by watching what we do than by listening to what we say.

What patterns are your children picking up from you? Are there patterns in your life that you wish you could hide from your children?

Dad comes home one night wringing his hands, complaining about his job, and blaming everyone else for something that has gone wrong in his department. The pattern that the children learn is to blame everyone else and never accept responsibility. That is not a pattern the Lord wants children to learn.

Let's look at a different example. Mother is facing a difficult situation at work. Father is deceased, and she has three children to raise alone. She may lose her job, and she is concerned about it, but what does she do? She gets the children together and says, "Let me tell you what is happening. I may lose my job, and you know we need it to make ends meet. I want us to pray together about Mom's job. Let's ask the Lord if He wants me to lose this one so that He can give me something better." She is building into them a beautiful pattern of life. When things get tough or you do not know which way to turn, you turn to God. Her children will never forget her example.

One time I asked my children, "Can you think of something that you learned from me because you watched my example?" Becky spoke right up and said, "When a problem arises, you pray about it. You ask the Lord to give you direction. You wait for His answer. You trust Him to give you the answer. Then you thank Him for it. You obey Him, whatever He says."

Long before my children were born, Anna and I prayed, "God teach me how to teach my children to pray and to trust You." I have made mistakes and have had my share of failures. I would like to have erased them so that my children would never know. But they have seen the mistakes and the failures too. Yet I know I did succeed in teaching them these two important principles, to pray and to trust. I overheard Andy tell someone that prayer had always been important in our family. He said, "I can remember walking in on Daddy many times early in the morning and finding him praying. I can remember how often he told me he prayed for me before I awakened each morning."

When was the last time your children heard you call

their names in prayer except around the table in a hurried-up blessing? When was the last time you said to them, "Why don't we talk to God and ask Him to show us what to do about this problem"? It makes no difference what you *tell* them. They learn more from what you *do*.

Imagine the following situation: The family is attending the worship service. The offering plate comes by, and Dad puts in a few dollars. The next Sunday Dad puts in nothing. What does that say to his children? The children grow up thinking that some Sundays they are to give to God and some Sundays it is not really necessary.

As you have been reading, perhaps you have thought about some experiences in your own life—behavior you wish your children had never seen or heard; other actions you hope they saw clearly and will never forget. You make these principles stick by being an example. We are not going to be perfect; we are all going to fail. But you must try to provide the best pattern you can for your children because it will have a profound effect on them.

Something happened not long ago that really made an impression on me. A bridegroom and his best man (who was his father) met me in my study to fill out the marriage license. While I was busy with the license, I noticed that the young man put his arm around his dad and hugged him. While we waited at the door before entering the sanctuary, the young man put his arm around his dad and hugged him again. Then they were both peeping through the window at the door to see their friends and family who had gathered. I noticed that father and son had their arms around each other. I was really moved by their actions. I think I learned something about the way that father raised his son. The young man had seen the loving example set by his father, and he had picked up on it and was carrying it with him into his new life with his new wife.

It makes no difference how many times children attend Sunday school and hear sermons. There is nothing under God's heaven like a mother and a father patterning principles they believe in if they want to hand those principles down to their children.

Persistence

Third, we hand down our faith by *persistence*. We pass it on by hanging in there and doing what needs to be done when it is convenient and when it is inconvenient. By repeating things over and over and over again, by living out the pattern over and over again. By being consistent in our responses to life's circumstances, we teach our children.

You can teach your children about honesty from the time they are infants. But if you brag about getting extra change back from the cashier at the grocery store, you have undermined your efforts and canceled out your integrity. You have etched into the minds of your children an inconsistency between what you say and what you do.

Paul said that we must "not grow weary while doing good, for in due season we shall reap if we do not lose heart" (Galatians 6:9). If we day by day by day exemplify and share principles in keeping with God's Word, we impress upon our children what they will carry into adulthood. That is why it is so vital to be consistent and persistent in what we teach.

Participation

Fourth, we hand down our faith by *participation*. Something positive happens when we get involved in what concerns or interests our children. We establish a caring relationship that makes it easier for us to communicate with them and teach them.

Your son comes home one day and tells you about a real problem he has at school. If you say, "Well, you are big enough to take care of that by yourself," what you are really saying is that you do not have time to get involved in his life. You are also communicating that you do not really value him as a person or care about him. You are depriving that son of the wisdom, experience, and knowledge you have to deal with his problem.

Your children may voice some opinions that you have trouble accepting. But you should not express your disagreement or your displeasure in terms that alienate your children. If you are going to hand down your faith, you must be open to listen to your children. You must be willing to be open to hear what they are *really* saying. They may be way off in left field in what they are thinking, but if you say, "Shame on you; you ought to know better than that," they will never feel free to share their honest thoughts with you again. Be open enough to listen to their viewpoints.

Your children may be totally wrong in their viewpoint, but you are not going to convince them otherwise by attacking them and telling them how wrong they are and how they should be ashamed of themselves. Taking the approach, saying, "Well, that is interesting. Tell me how you arrived at that," will establish an atmosphere that is not threatening but is conducive to the sharing of ideas.

When we get involved in the lives and the thinking of our children, we are able to convey to them and build into them the kind of faith that they need. But if we shut them out and they feel that we really do not care, that we just want them to do what we say to do, we have no chance of passing on to them our faith. We can only hand down our faith to children who are receptive to it.

We must participate in their problems by being with them and saying to them that we know how they feel. Admitting that we have failed too binds us to our children. We become individuals who are not perfect who also make mistakes. Then we can tell them we have learned some principles we would be willing to share if they would like.

How do we hand down our faith? By getting in there where out children are hurting and showing them how to apply the principles that we have learned.

Praise

The greatest motivation in the world for learning is *praise*. That is the fifth way we hand down our faith. We all like and appreciate praise. So why should our children be any different? We always seem to have time to tell our children what they have done wrong, but I think it is perhaps more important for us to take each opportunity to tell them what they have done right.

If you want your children to do the right things, praise them for even the smallest things they do right. Your son comes home and tells you that he only made an eighty-four on his history test. How do you respond? Do you say, "You should have at least made ninety"? He could have made sixty, so praise him for what he did do. Perhaps you could say, "That is not a bad grade at all, is it? I am proud of you for making a passing grade." If you think he could do better (or if he seems to be displeased with his grade), you could ask him if he is having any problems with the subject and then volunteer to help him. That is the way to motivate children, not by trying to shame them into doing better.

Let's look at another example of how to praise. Your teenage daughter is having a problem and comes to you for advice. Instead of telling her exactly what to do, you go together to God's Word to see what He has to say about the problem. Then when she applies what she has learned, you praise her for having the courage to do what she knows is in keeping with God's instruction. By doing this, you build her confidence and reassure her that you are on her side and that you trust her to behave responsibly. Positive praise is great motivation for righteous doing.

If you want to hand down your faith, praise your children for all the good they do. They are going to make mistakes, and your positive response will be a great opportunity of growth for them.

Prayer

The last idea I want to discuss is *prayer*. By placing this subject last in our discussion does not mean it is the last thing we are to do in handing down our faith. I think our prayers should be a part of each of the previous ideas we have examined.

God answers the prayers of godly parents who want to raise godly children. Parents who spend time praying for their children, and praying with their children, demonstrate the importance of prayer. And they establish the right kind of pattern for their children.

Paul wrote that we are to "pray without ceasing" (1 Thessalonians 5:17) and to continue "steadfastly in prayer" (Romans 12:12), and that is certainly the example Jesus set for us. He prayed prayers in all kinds of situations. We can do no less as examples for our children.

A FAITH TO SUSTAIN CHILDREN

Do you have a faith that is worth handing down? If you hand down your faith the way you are living it now, will your children be the better for having received and accepted your lifestyle? If you have never trusted Jesus Christ as your personal Savior, what will you have to leave them? Will it be a life of indifference and rebellion? It may be a very sophisticated and socially acceptable life, but a life of indifference and disobedience to Him.

If you are a godly parent, look at what you have to give to your children. You may not be able to leave them even a small amount of money but if you loved God and practiced the principles of Scripture, if you have loved your children and listened to them, you will leave them a faith to sustain them through every difficulty, every heartache, and every trial of life.

My challenge to you is to build a strong Christian home.

You do that by handing down your faith in the ways I have suggested here. If you will purpose to do so, you will keep your kids on your team.

I leave you with this prayer:

Father, thank You for the wonderful truths of Your Word. I pray that the Holy Spirit will take these truths and seal them in the heart of every father and every mother, recognizing that they are for the protection of the family, both in the present and in the future. Let nothing take priority over our awesome responsibility as godly parents.

APPLYING PRINCIPLE SIX

1. Identify elements of your faith that you would like to hand down to your children.

2. What principles of Scripture have especially influenced your thinking?

3. Have you thought of some experiences in your life that you hope your children will never forget? What are they? Ask your children if they remember any of the ones that you think have been significant.

4. Have you been able to be persistent and consistent in teaching your children? If you answered no, why not? If you answered yes, why do you think that is true?

5. In the past, have you been open to listen to your children's opinions? Perhaps you need to rethink your

approach in this area. Pay particular attention to your attitude the next time you have a conversation with one of your children.

6. Try to think of some daily situations in which you can praise your children, and then follow through by praising them.

7. Do you "pray without ceasing" for your children? For your family as a whole?

SEVEN

PROVIDING FOR
YOUR CHILDREN

ADEQUATELY PROVIDING FOR THE FAMILY HAS always been a challenge, but in recent years it seems that the task has become even greater. That is why I want to address this chapter to everyone who is the head of a household. As you will see by the following statements, I include both men and women in this category. Of course both parents will gain by understanding the ideas presented here, so I encourage both to read about this subject.

According to the United States Census Bureau figures, there were 97,000,000 families in our country in 1994. Of that number, 2,910,000 were maintained by a man with no wife present, and 17,460,000 were maintained by a woman with no husband present. That is a sizable number of people, especially women, who are having to make a living and raise children alone. These single parents deserve our special prayers and consideration because they are having to do the job of two people.

A BIBLICAL COMMAND

Would you consider yourself to be an excellent provider, a good provider, an adequate provider, or a poor provider? Your answer will certainly be affected by what you think is involved in being a provider for your family. Here is what Paul said about the subject:

> But if anyone does not provide for his own, and especially for those of his household, he has denied the faith and is worse than an unbeliever.
>
> —*1 Timothy 5:8*

That was a strong statement for him to make to the Christians with Timothy at Ephesus. How can anyone deny the faith by not providing for the household? How can anyone be worse than an unbeliever?

Paul did not mean that someone who denied the faith was lost, having once been saved. He meant that the person denied by attitude, action, or conduct a very clearly given biblical principle to provide for the family.

Many people in many cultures today make no profession of being Christian; they do not believe in Jesus Christ or in our God. But they have laws that concern providing for and taking care of parents and other members of the family. I am sure that you know unsaved people who have a clear understanding of their responsibility to provide for their families. These unbelievers are better providers than Christians who fail to provide for their families. That is what Paul meant by being worse than an unbeliever.

MEETING THE NEEDS

When has the head of the household genuinely provided for the family, especially the children? To answer that, I think we need to look at three important needs in our lives—material, emotional, and spiritual—and see how the head of the household meets each need.

Material Needs

Let's begin where most of us usually begin, and that is in providing for material needs. Everyone requires food, clothing, and shelter. When God says we are to provide, He means we are to provide for these basic needs. We may not always be able to provide everything that everybody in the family would like to have, but that is different from what they *need*.

The problem is this: Some heads of household think they have done their job when they have provided materially for their families. But they have not completed the job when they have done that. For example, someone who has a sizable income can provide everything the family needs and wants, but a good provider will not give them *every-thing* they want. A good provider will not fulfill every desire. There must be some limitations.

If a child makes a request, that request may be unwise if it results in a lack of discipline or a lack of self-control. The teenager who begs for a sports car and promptly receives one may be tempted to drive too fast, stay out too late, or go to unauthorized places. A wise provider might help the teenager buy a vehicle that affords basic transportation—no frills or fancy extras—until the teenager learns how to handle the responsibility that comes with driving and owning a car. The teenager may not need a car at all, and the wise provider takes that into consideration too.

Our son's first car was used. We found one we thought would be practical. Dependable. We made the down payment and let him make the monthly payments. In looking back now, he agrees that our decision was the best one—although he didn't necessarily think so at the time. In fact, it wasn't until he was in seminary that I went out and bought him the car he wanted. He has thanked me many times for waiting.

Parents who have plenty of money may give their children everything they need and most of what they want in order to boost their own personal pride and standing in society. For example, a father who sees to it that his children always have the most expensive clothes, always drive fine automobiles, and always have more than enough money may be trying to impress his neighbors, his friends, and his coworkers. That is not the proper motivation for providing for children.

There is another aspect of the problem of pride in regard

to providing material possessions. Some husbands insist that their wives work so that they can have more and better possessions than their friends or neighbors. As a result of the need to have "more," both the husband and the wife may work harder and harder, longer and longer hours, to keep up with the payments on all their possessions. What happens to the children in the meantime? They may have the biggest house on the block, but it may also be the loneliest house, not a real home as it should be. Children need their parents and their parents' love and attention more than they need "more" things. It is difficult to keep your children on your team if you are never with them.

I realize that there are times when a wife has to work, and I am sure God understands that. And as I have said earlier, a single parent has to work to provide for the family. I am not talking about those kinds of situations. However, I do not think God excuses situations such as those I have just described when things take precedence over children. The head of the household is going to be held accountable to God for such selfishness.

Before I leave this section on material needs, I must say a few words about what I think makes a poor provider. Here I address only men. The poor provider cannot keep a job because he does not want a job. He is unwilling to do anything to provide for the family's needs, and he forces his wife to get a job to keep the family going. I have no doubt that God hates slothfulness, and any man who marries a woman and treats her in this fashion does not deserve her. Lazy husbands put awesome burdens on wives that God never intended for them to bear. I think it is better for a man not to marry than to willingly fail to assume the responsibility before God to provide for his family's material needs.

Emotional Needs

We are also responsible for providing for our family's emotional needs. What exactly is involved in meeting emotional needs? I could simply say that the household head is to provide love for the family, but that is not a very helpful explanation. The word *love* has many meanings, and one person's understanding of what it means can be vastly different from another person's. To solve the problem and to prevent misunderstanding, I have determined that at least three things should be conveyed to children in meeting their emotional needs. The good or excellent provider is one who builds into children a sense of belonging, a sense of worthiness, and a sense of confidence.

When someone says, "I love my kids. Look how I provide for them," we probably need to look closely at the relationship with the children. If the household head provides material things to get the children out of the way and never spends time with them, that person is a poor provider of emotional needs. But if the parent relates well to the children, is intimately involved with them, and enjoys with them the material wealth that God has given, that person does show love for the children and is being a good provider for emotional needs.

A *sense of belonging* is the first feeling that should be conveyed to children. Everyone needs to feel a sense of belonging, a sense of being accepted and wanted in the family. If you are going to build stability and strength and security within children, you need to make them feel a part of the family.

Children who are not made to feel that they belong feel rejected. It is painful and emotionally destructive for children to sit around the same table with other family members, eat the same food, but feel shut out of the family circle. Criticism, indifference, or direct statements by the father can communicate to children that they were never wanted. If you remember, we talked about this subject earlier in the book, and we looked at how damaging such things can be to children.

Feelings of rejection can cause children to seek acceptance elsewhere. A young man may respond by running away from home and joining some group willing to accept him as he is. But such a group may take advantage of the young person's desperate need to belong and require him to participate in some harmful activity. A young woman may respond by leaving home at an early age to get married. But she has no true picture of what marriage is all about, and she ends up getting a divorce. For the rest of her life she carries with her a deep desire to belong that may never be fulfilled. Another young person may react by becoming totally self-centered, asserting his own importance and denouncing the need for others in his life. He develops an attitude of "me" first and "me" only. In each of these cases, the young person is set up to be an unhappy, unfulfilled adult.

The parent needs to help the children get the "we" feeling. That is a very strong feeling of loyalty to the family, a feeling of oneness, the feeling of being a part of the family. It is a vital part of growing a strong family unit and fulfilling a basic emotional need.

The second feeling that needs to be conveyed to children

is a *sense of worthiness*. Children who have a sense of worthiness know that they are valued and treasured as God's gifts to the family.

Children need a sense of worth within the family and also before others and before God. If you have communicated your unconditional love and acceptance to your children, you have helped build up their sense of worth within the family. Your positive responses to them reassure them of their worth to you, and they can carry this sense of self-esteem with them as they interact with others—in school, at church, in clubs, and in other social settings. We discussed in Chapter 6 ways of handing down your faith. If you are successful in doing this, your children will have a clear idea of their worth to God and of the importance of serving Him according to His principles. Because willful disobedience to God chisels away at a person's sense of self-worth, the parent needs to teach the children the importance of being obedient to God.

The third thing that must be conveyed to children is a *sense of competence*. Competent children can say, "I can do it. I am able. I am adequate. I am equipped to handle this situation."

By encouraging our children, we tell them that we believe in them and we know that they are going to do their best. This kind of support will fire children's enthusiasm and bolster their self-confidence.

Destructive messages, such as "You won't ever amount to anything" or "You can't do anything right," are indelibly impressed on the minds of children, and they carry those messages with them into adulthood. How can children desire to be on your team if they think you have no confidence in them?

Confidence breeds confidence, and negative comments breed negative thoughts. Children can be so overwhelmed by thoughts of their unworthiness, their failure in their parents' eyes, that they can be emotionally damaged for life. The only hope they have is to undergo a transforming experience by Christ in their lives and thus gain an understanding of who they really are in Jesus Christ.

Can you look back in your childhood and think of anything that was said or done to you by a parent that made an indelible negative impression on you? I would guess that many people have some such recollection. The parent may not have meant to do it or say it, but it happened anyway. As a result, something entered your thinking about your inadequacy in some area.

Now look back in your childhood and think of something that was said to you, some word of encouragement, that left you feeling good about yourself. You probably do not ever want to forget it because the experience was so highly motivating.

Why do I ask you about your childhood experiences? Because you need to look back and evaluate what you were taught, why you were taught it, how your parents behaved toward you, and why you had certain successes and failures. If you do not do that, you will probably repeat with your children the same mistakes your parents made with you. Evaluate your past in light of your sense of belonging, your sense of worthiness, and your sense of confidence. Did your parents convey those feelings to you?

I know from experience that many parents grew up in family environments in which men did not hug each other, dads not hug their sons, and people were generally not very expressive emotionally. That made a difference, and the society in which you and I live is suffering as a result. One thing about this present-day generation is that we are more expressive emotionally, and that is good. Men hug men in genuine Christlike love for each other. Sons hug their fathers. I can remember when Andy was about fifteen, and I walked up to him and gave him a big hug and told him how much I loved him. He shrugged me off. I reminded him "You will never get too old for your daddy to hug you."

Parents and children should show outward affection and not be afraid to say, "I love you." Such relationships reaffirm children's worth and instill in them a sense of belonging and a sense of confidence. The good provider will endeavor to see that these things are provided for their children. If they do not grow up with these feelings, they may become adults burdened by emotional deficiency.

A little boy who has been filled with negative thoughts about himself may become the thirty-two-year-old man who is still trying to prove to his parents that he is worth something, that he does have a place in this world. He may become a multimillionaire, and the little boy inside the fifty-year-old man is still trying to prove to his parents that he can do it. And even at sixty and seventy years of age, he may still be trying, even though his parents have been dead for years. You can help your children avoid such a tragic adulthood by providing for their emotional needs in keeping with what God directs.

PROVIDING FOR YOUR CHILDREN

Spiritual Needs

The third area to be provided for is the spiritual. We are all spiritual beings. One day we are going to stand before the living God to give an account of our lives.

How can you be a good provider and provide materially and emotionally for your children and not provide for them the one thing that is absolutely essential in this life and the life to come? Are you trying to provide for your children while you are living in disobedience and rebellion toward God? If you are, you are teaching your children to think you do not need God. The children may think that if you do not need Him, they do not need Him, either. That is no example to set for them. (We will discuss this subject in more detail in a later chapter.)

If you want to provide well for your children, here is the first step: Ask God to forgive you of your sin, and receive Jesus Christ as your personal Savior. Be willing to change your attitude about the way you have been thinking and then turn your life over to God. Ask Him to guide you and lead you. If you want to be a good provider, you must start with Jesus Christ who enables you to provide spiritual leadership for your family.

If you are already a Christian, some of this advice may not really apply to you. But as a Christian, you have the responsibility of explaining to your children how to be saved. You say, "That is the pastor's responsibility." No, it is not his alone. It is one of his responsibilities, to be sure, but it is primarily your responsibility. You are the head of your family, and your children are subject to you spiritually before they are subject to the pastor. You are the one who is responsible. If you are unsure about the best way to present this topic to your children, ask your pastor for advice. He will be happy to explain to you in terms you can use with your children.

Some people will probably disagree with what I am about to say next, but I believe it is in keeping with biblical teaching. If a godly father asks for permission to baptize a son or a daughter he has led to Christ, I happily answer yes. Nothing in the Bible says that pastors are the only ones who can baptize others.

Think about it for a moment. Think about that child standing ready for baptism, and he hears his father say, "I baptize you in the name of the Father, the Son, and the Holy Spirit." That is an experience the child will never forget. I cannot help thinking it will be more meaningful to him.

I believe that a godly father in a Bible-believing church should have the privilege to baptize his children if he desires to do so. Notice that I said a godly father, not a perfect father. I simply mean a man whose testimony is above question. He loves the Lord and is trying to build a Christian family and keep his kids on his team. What greater joy could a father have than to baptize his own children?

THE GREAT PROVIDER

God is the Great Provider. Because He saw that we needed to belong, He allowed us to become a part of His family. As Christians, we are members of the family of God. We are the children of God, the body of Christ.

God saw that we needed a sense of worthiness, so what did he do? He sent His only begotten Son to the cross, and Jesus paid the awful price for our sin. How worthy and valuable are we to God? Look to the Cross and the blood of His only begotten Son. They are everlasting proof that we are worth something to almighty God.

Then God saw that we needed to feel confident. What did he do? He sent the Holy Spirit who is our Great Enabler. He makes it possible for us to achieve and accomplish anything and everything that is the will of the Father. And so we live every day indwelt by the Great Enabler, the Holy Spirit.

Where does that place us? That places us in a position of being well provided for by the Father. We belong to the kingdom, we are purchased by the Cross, and we are filled with the Spirit. God has provided for all our needs.

My mother has said to me, "I regret that I couldn't give you the things other parents gave to their children." And I have answered her, "Mom, you have nothing to regret. You gave me something that is not for sale in any store, has never been manufactured, and cannot be purchased anywhere. You planted within me a love for God, a desire to be obedient, a desire to be willing to stand, regardless of other people's opinions or attitudes, to do what is right. You taught me to depend upon God for everything. You taught me how to pray. You taught me to trust God as my faithful Father." I would rather have my meager possessions as a child—two pairs of bib overalls, one pair of shoes, a couple of pairs of socks, some underwear, a toothbrush, and a comb combined with what my mom taught me—than all the wealth the world can offer.

It is not how many things you provide for your children. It is what you give them of yourself and the principles of Scripture that can never be taken away. If you are a good provider, you will keep your children on your team and will establish a firm foundation for them as adults.

APPLYING PRINCIPLE SEVEN

1. In light of our discussion here, are you a good provider or a poor provider for your children? Or are there areas in which you are a good provider and other areas in which you are a poor provider?

2. Have you been so caught up in trying to provide for your family's material needs that you have neglected their emotional and spiritual needs?

3. How can you help your children feel a sense of belonging?

4. In what ways can you convey a sense of worthiness to them?

5. Do your children have a sense of confidence? Can you think of some experiences in their lives that illustrate their feelings of confidence?

6. Can you recall some positive and negative childhood experiences that made indelible impressions on your mind? How can you learn from them so that you can reproduce the successes and not the failures with your children?

EIGHT

TEACHING YOUR CHILDREN THE IMPORTANCE OF PRAYER

WHEN THE PLAYERS ON A FOOTBALL TEAM GET into a huddle on the field, they receive their play from the team captain who in turn has received it from the coach. As a result of these agreed-upon instructions, the players can know the plan of action and act as a team. Imagine the havoc on the football field if each person played the game only as he wanted to, failing to follow the coach's instructions, thereby ruining the team's attempt for a successful game. So it is when parents fail to teach children how to pray. It is through prayer that they discover the plays to be carried out during the game of life the great Coach of heaven has planned for them.

Some of you may be thinking, *I don't know enough about prayer to get answers from God for myself, much less about how to teach my kids to pray.* Remember, we have been talking about the family as a team. If you and your spouse have not been praying together, you need to discuss this and make a commitment to start working on being a team as a family with praying together as one of your major goals.

As I have counseled some couples on this subject of praying out loud together, they had to admit that they knew so little about getting started that they would probably have to "pool their ignorance" in order to learn. Don't get bogged down with the mechanics of praying; just do it. It is really just talking out loud to God, just as you would talk to a very good friend. In reality, that is exactly what you are doing, talking to your Very Best Friend. As adults, we may feel foolish talking to Someone we cannot see, but God is always present even though we cannot see Him. Small children do not usually have a problem with this idea at all.

Why Pray Together?

It was Augustine who said, "Love is not looking at each other, but looking in the same direction." There is a sense in which prayer could be defined in the same terms. In prayer we are forced to take our minds off all those around us and concentrate on the heavenly Father and our relationship with Him.

Encourage your children

to pray about decisions

concerning their

standards and values

as well as their behavior.

As you pray together as a family, you will be developing a family unity that no problems or storms later on can destroy. As you pray, you will all be focusing your attention in the same direction toward God who wants to bless His children, especially the family unit, more than you could ever imagine. The Bible tells us that since the beginning of time, people have not seen, heard, or perceived all that God has prepared for "the one who waits for Him" (Isaiah 64:4). It is a very good thing to wait on the Lord in prayer and to teach our children to do the same.

When my children were very small, I used Kenneth Taylor's book *The Bible in Pictures for Little Eyes* (Chicago: Moody, 1956) at night when I put them to bed and prayed with them. One of their favorite stories was about Samuel and about his hearing God's voice speaking to him at night. They thought it was funny each time Samuel got up and asked Eli if he had called for him. As the story became more and more familiar, they would sometimes giggle because they knew who was really calling to Samuel. As a result of this and other Bible stories, they learned early in life that God really speaks to His children.

I don't remember their asking about how God speaks; they just grew up believing that He speaks to those who are listening. You should encourage your children to pray about decisions concerning their standards and values as well as their behavior. If this is to happen, your children will need to know how to pray and realize the importance of prayer in their daily lives. Without learning to pray and to depend wholly upon God for everything, they will continue to look to someone else to meet their needs and answer their questions. At first, they will probably look to you, their parents. Later, especially if things go bad at home, they will look to their peers for direction only to find their friends are as much without direction as they are. Then where do they go? Maybe some will seek good and helpful counsel from a mature Christian. But too often the young people who have no background for making wise and godly decisions think they are accountable only to themselves.

BUT HOW DO I DO IT?

Many times my children would open my study door and see me stretched out on the floor praying. Most of the time they would close the door quietly and leave. Sometimes, though, Andy or Becky would come in, tiptoe over to where I was, and stretch out beside me. Andy wouldn't say anything, but Becky would wait for a while and then whisper, "Dad, I have a little problem. Could we pray about it together?" I have always believed that two of the most important things I could ever teach them were the importance of prayer and how to pray. I guess the old saying, I'd rather see a sermon than hear one any day, is still true. My children probably could not tell you much of what I have said in sermons on prayer (and I have preached a lot on the subject), but they have both told me that they will never forget seeing me stretched out before God, talking to Him about whatever was on my heart. So I know that the best way you can teach your kids to pray is by your example.

PRAY TOGETHER AS A FAMILY

When major decisions of the family had to be made, we prayed together about them. Relocating in the pastorate was one that always seemed to require extra prayers and special consideration. One of the most difficult decisions we ever had to make was to leave Florida and come to Atlanta. We loved Florida and the warm climate. We loved our town and the church we served there. We had made many dear, close friends, and we really did not want to move. Oh! How we all prayed and prayed and then prayed some more.

During this time of deciding, we would talk about it in between the prayer sessions. One evening, after it seemed clear that we would be moving, we were all four riding our bicycles after supper. Andy and I were a little ahead of Anna and Becky. We were all being quiet and just enjoying the peace and quiet of that little community when Andy broke the silence and said, "Dad, it's not always easy to obey God, is it?"

I answered, "No."

Then he said, "But, you know, every time we do, God always blesses us."

He was barely eleven years old, and tears came to my eyes as I realized how wise he was for his age and what an important thing he was learning, to pray and find the mind of God in all decisions, both small and great.

Pray with Children Individually

In Chapter 3 I talked about showing an interest in your children's daily experiences. One of the best ways to demonstrate how much you really care about what is going on in their lives is to pray with them about their individual problems. When Becky was in high school, she was asked to be in the Miss Teenage Georgia Pageant. At first she was excited, then she would worry about it, and then she would doubt she had made the right decision about being in it at all. We were with her each step of the way. We discussed it at breakfast time, dinnertime, bedtime-snack time, and any other time we were together. She was having a tough time making up her mind about what to do. Anna and I told her we were supportive of any decision she chose to make. Of course, I told her she was sure to win the title if she entered, but she was not sure she wanted to win or even be in it.

After much prayer and discussion, she decided that she would participate. So she and Anna went shopping for just the right pageant dress. They decided to look for a long white dress, and they prayed that God would show them the exact dress to buy that would not cost more than we could afford to pay. (You can tell that we believe at our house that nothing is too big or too little to pray about.) They had not looked long before they turned the corner at one of the shopping malls and saw the very dress they both had dreamed of on a mannequin in a store window. It was five minutes before closing time for the store, so they went in quickly to ask about the size and the price of the dress. Anna asked the manager if he would have the dress ready for Becky to try on the next afternoon after school. He agreed, and they came home elated over God's answer to prayer about a dress.

Then the time came for the pageant itself. Becky prayed only that she would bring glory to God in and through it all, and we prayed for her throughout the hours of the event. We were so proud of her.

When the finalists were named, Becky was one of them, and we cheered her on from the audience. Each finalist was brought on stage individually to answer a question so that the judges could see how well she could respond spontaneously. We knew Becky would be last because the finalists were called in alphabetical order, so we listened to hear each question and how each girl answered.

The first girl was asked if she could have any car she wanted, which car she would choose and why. The second girl was asked what flower she would choose to be and why. Andy was sitting beside me and almost groaned, "I wonder how Becky is going to bring glory to God with those kinds of questions?" So we bowed our heads and prayed that Becky would get a question she could glorify God with. The third girl had to choose which animal she would be, and I forget what the fourth had to choose.

Finally, it was Becky's turn. She looked so beautiful and radiant in that long white dress as she approached the center of the stage. We were still praying when the judge asked his question, and we nearly shouted for joy when we heard it. He said, "Becky, if you could choose any holiday, which would you choose and why?" We were really praising the Lord this time.

Becky stepped up to that microphone without a moment's hesitation and announced for the whole world to hear, "I would choose Easter, because that's when we celebrate the death, burial, and resurrection of our Lord Jesus Christ. And I know He is alive today, because He lives in me." The whole audience stood up and cheered, and we cried and hugged each other and clapped along with everyone else. We didn't care if Becky won or not, but we surely were proud that she was our daughter. Nobody will ever convince the Stanley family that God doesn't answer prayer. This is just one of the many times the Lord has answered our prayers concerning our children.

ENCOURAGE THEM TO HAVE THEIR OWN QUIET TIME

Notice that I said "encourage" them, not browbeat them or take away their privileges if they don't. If you have set the example and have had times of family prayer together and your children have grown accustomed to God's answering prayer, it will be natural for them to set aside some time alone to talk to God and to read His Word. Of course, I am assuming that your children have a personal relationship with the Lord if they are old enough to have made this commitment. If they are still young, allow God to work in His own time about this decision. However, if they are already in their teens, they need to consider making a decision to receive Jesus Christ into their lives and to commit themselves to Him. Ask the Lord for direction about how to deal with this matter.

ANSWERED PRAYER

In teaching our children to pray, we encouraged them to pray about anything that concerned them. When Becky was about three years old, an elderly couple lived next door to us. Becky loved them and would often go with me to visit them. One day the wife fell and broke her hip. She was in the hospital for a long time, and when she came home, she had to walk with crutches. Becky was concerned for her so she would include the woman in her prayers every night. As an adult, I'm not sure I really thought the elderly woman would ever be restored to full health again, but I did not discourage Becky from praying for her night after night to be able to walk again without those crutches. Late one night after Becky had been asleep for hours, the husband called me to say that his wife had just passed away. Oh, this Daddy did not know how his little girl would react to such sad news.

I had to leave the task of telling her to her mother because I had an early appointment the next day. It was Becky's first experience with death. Anna prayed alone before she told Becky, for she knew how important it was for Becky's faith that this be handled God's way. As Becky was waking up, Anna went in, sat on the edge of her bed, and began talking to her about their plans for the day. Then she simply told Becky that last night her elderly friend had gone home to be with Jesus. The child surprised her mother by reacting with a big smile and great joy, exclaiming, "Oh, Mother, isn't that wonderful! Jesus will give her some new legs, and she won't need those old crutches anymore." How we underestimate the faith of little children! For Becky, her prayers were answered; her elderly friend who used to give her candy would have a brand-new pair of legs.

Don't ever be afraid of what your children pray. Just teach them that God does not always answer the way we want, but He does always answer. If you really want to keep your kids on your team, you must teach them to pray. I want to stress the importance of praying with your children, starting when they are young, but if they are older, *start today*. It is never too late to start.

APPLYING PRINCIPLE EIGHT

1. Pray together as a family.

2. Set the example by making every matter a subject of prayer.

3. Pray with individual family members.

4. Encourage a daily quiet time.

5. Draw your family's attention to answered prayer.

NINE

TEACHING YOUR CHILDREN
TO WHOM THEY ARE
ULTIMATELY RESPONSIBLE

$\backsim$

AS I BEGAN TO OUTLINE THE CHAPTERS FOR
this book, I asked my children what they thought made the
biggest impact on their lives in terms of their commitment
to the Lord and to our family. My son was quick to answer.
He said that he did not rebel against his mother and me for
any length of time because he knew in his heart he was ultimately responsible to God, not to us. He believes that this
one principle above all the others is the key to keeping your
kids on your team.

SOMEBODY'S WATCHING

When I talk about being responsible to somebody, I mean having to answer to that person. As children grow up, they find they must answer to their parents. Parents make the rules, and children are expected to abide by them. Initially, their experience tells them that they are ultimately responsible to their parents.

Children quickly learn that if they can successfully hide their inappropriate actions from their parents, they are not held responsible or accountable for those actions. And often they do succeed in keeping things from us; we do not always know what they have and have not done. Thus, in their minds, they "get by" with things.

In reality, however, no one "gets by" with anything. Scripture is clear that each of us will give an account to God of our actions:

> We shall stand before the judgment
> seat of Christ.
> For it is written:
> "As I live, says the LORD,
> Every knee shall bow to Me,
> And every tongue shall confess to God."
> So then each of us shall give account of himself
> to God.
> —*Romans 14:10–12*

Unfortunately, many parents fail to communicate this to their children. They fail to transfer their children's sense of accountability from themselves to God. As a result, their children grow up thinking that when Mom and Dad don't see what they do, and when their other earthly authorities do not see what they do, they have gotten away with something. Consequently, an attitude develops that says, "I am only wrong when I get caught." This is not an unusual attitude among individuals in detention centers and prisons across our country. I believe it starts in the home.

Who Is in Charge, Anyway?

The biblical concept that serves as the basis of this principle is found in Romans 13:1–7:

> Let every soul be subject to the governing authorities. For there is no authority except from God, and the authorities that exist are appointed by God. Therefore whoever resists the authority resists the ordinance of God, and those who resist will bring judgment on themselves. For rulers are not a terror to good works, but to evil. Do you want to be unafraid of the authority? Do what is good, and you will have praise from the same. For he is God's minister to you for good. But if you do evil, be afraid; for he does not bear the sword in vain; for he is God's minister, an avenger to execute wrath on him who practices evil. Therefore you must be subject, not only because of wrath but also for conscience' sake. For because of this you also pay taxes, for they are God's ministers attending continually to this very thing.

Render therefore to all their due: taxes to whom taxes are due, customs to whom customs, fear to whom fear, honor to whom honor.

Here Paul teaches that all authority is ultimately from God. Although the specific application of the principle in this case is governmental authority, the principle has much broader implications. Passages such as "Children, obey your parents in the Lord, for this is right" (Ephesians 6:1) and "Children, obey your parents in all things, for this is well pleasing to the Lord" (Colossians 3:20) make it clear that this principle applies to the authority structure in the family as well.

The punch line of the Romans 13 passage is found in verse 2: "Therefore whoever resists the authority resists the ordinance of God, and those who resist will bring judgment on themselves." Basically, Paul is saying that since God is ultimately behind all established authority, to disobey one's earthly authorities is to disobey God. Therefore, every time we deal with authority, we deal with God. In essence, we are ultimately responsible to God. Thus, it is only right that on Judgment Day we will have to give an account to Him of all we have done, regardless of what we got by with in regard to our earthly authorities.

A NECESSARY PROCESS

Helping your children transfer their feelings of responsibility from you to God is a process. As we will see, it is a process that entails some risk, some pain, and great faith. But before we get into that, you must understand that this process must begin early in the lives of children. There are two reasons for this.

First of all, *children need to make this transfer in an environment of acceptance and love,* an environment to which they feel free to return when they have been wrong. Since part of the process of teaching this principle is a gradual increase in your children's freedom, there is a certain failure factor to take into account. They will need a place to regroup when they fail, especially when they experience their first failures in decision making and discernment, and I believe the home is the best place for them to find the security they need at that point.

For instance, it is far better for a young lady to have the freedom to make a mistake about the type of guy she dates while still at home than to have that decision made for her until she leaves home. Or worse, for her to have to secretly see a certain fellow, discover her parents were right about him, and then not be able to turn to them for help for fear of retaliation.

When my son was in high school, he began playing in rock bands. This was certainly not my first preference for how he spent his spare time, but I believed he had a sensitive conscience toward the Lord and I left the decision with him. As I talked with him about the events surrounding his eventual departure from that scene, some interesting things surfaced.

He admitted knowing the whole time that playing in a rock band was not God's best for him. He also pointed out that the mental turmoil he went through—arguing with God day and night—resulted not only in his finally quitting the band but also in his surrendering his life to full-time Christian service.

The thing that really hit me, however, was his statement, "Knowing you and Mom were waiting at home with open and accepting arms made it much easier to face the rejection of the guys in the band and the kids at school when I told them I was quitting."

I am convinced that my stepping in and making him quit would have robbed him of this life-changing experience and would have damaged our relationship. I am equally convinced that his sensitive conscience was the product of several years of working to wean him from responsibility to Mom and Dad to responsibility to God.

A second reason this process must begin when children are young is that *the consequences of their wrong decisions will not be as great as they may be later on.* For instance, the consequences of your children's spending all their money on candy are much less traumatic than those of their going thousands of dollars in debt for possessions they cannot afford. Proper instruction in managing money, beginning with their allowances, can lessen their chances of making serious financial blunders as they enter adulthood. Also, the consequences of your children's choosing the wrong friends at age ten will be less damaging than those of their choosing the wrong friends at age eighteen.

I am not advocating that you relinquish complete control of your children's lives. This will become much clearer as you read further about this process.

WHEN DO I START?

There are three things to do when you involve your children in this process. First, you must encourage them to prayerfully set their own standards and parameters in certain areas. Second, you must allow them to follow through with what they believe God has shown them. Third, you must demonstrate a life of responsibility to God. The remainder of this chapter will examine each of these three aspects of the process in some depth.

Handing Them the Reins

The first thing you must do is this: *You must allow them to begin prayerfully setting what they believe to be God's standards for certain areas of their lives.* Begin with something simple, something harmless. For instance, instead of telling them what chores to do around the house, have them pray about it. Tell them to ask God to bring to their minds the things they could help with around the house. It is okay to give helpful suggestions, but do not steal their joy of discovery.

Instead of telling your children how to spend and save their money, have them pray about it. Have them ask God about how the allowance should be budgeted. Once that is settled in their minds they will be responsible to God for their money. They may fool you when they spend it all on something foolish, but their conscience will bother them and they will have made a giant step in understanding the principle of their ultimate responsibility.

Another example could be the study/play schedule. Have

them pray about when they should study and when they should play. Stress to them that God will bring to their minds what He wants them to do.

There are many other areas to which this principle could be applied. Most of them are things that we as parents naturally dictate to our children. In doing so, however, we rob them of opportunities to develop a sense of responsibility to God. I do not believe you can begin this process too soon. The sooner they view themselves as responsible to God, the better.

It is a tragedy when parents ignore this principle. Once their kids become teenagers, they seem to expect instant maturity, as if a certain age guaranteed a corresponding level of maturity. On the contrary, as children gain the freedoms that come with being teenagers (driving, dating, working, spending weekends away), they often make the most immature decisions of their lives. Why? They have had little or no experience in making decisions for themselves. And when they did, they were always responsible to Mom and Dad.

Do not be surprised if your children resist you the first time you try this. More than likely they will want you to make the decisions for them. That is what they are accustomed to. Yet it is this very dependency you are working to transfer to their heavenly Father. I am not saying that you are to be uninvolved in the growth and maturity of your children, that you are to ignore their questions and decisions. On the contrary, what I am suggesting will mean *more* involvement.

I remember when my son first became interested in goal

setting. He was in the tenth grade at the time. After giving him some tips, I sent him off to work alone. He worked for a little while, came back to me, and said, "You set goals for me." Frankly, it would have been much easier to do it for him. Back and forth we went. I would give him some hints; he would go away and work for a while. It became quite an ordeal for both of us. However, my giving in to him would have cheated him out of an opportunity to learn at an early age one of the keys to success in life. Now, as an adult, he is very goal oriented, both in his personal life and in his ministry. I cannot help believing that this is partially a result of this experience and other similar ones when I encouraged him to make decisions for himself.

It is much easier to make all your children's decisions for them than it is to work through them in the manner I am suggesting. It takes time, patience, and, as you will see, great faith. At times you will become frustrated, and you will be tempted to revert to simply dictating their standards and decisions. While they are children, that method will work fine. When they are older, however, and they are not as quick to respond positively to your every wish, this method will work to the detriment of you and your children and your relationship with each other.

A Painful Process

This shift in responsibility is a necessary process and usually a painful one as well. Sometimes parents must stand back and watch children make the wrong decisions. I believe the potential for pain hinders many parents from helping their children in this area. It is natural for parents to want to spare children from pain, yet this is a necessary risk if your children are to be ready for life and thus stay on your team.

And so we come to the second thing you must do in implementing this principle: *You must allow them to follow through with what they believe God has shown them.* That is, once you have encouraged them to prayerfully decide in an issue, you must allow them to follow through. To jump in and interfere at this point is to short-circuit the whole thing. You will be worse off than when you started. You will have communicated, "You are not capable of making the right decision." If in fact they made the wrong decision, experience will make that clear.

I will never forget the day my son asked us for permission to attend his first rock concert. It was to be held on a Sunday night. Being the pastor of the church, I knew that my decision could be a precedent-setting one. But there was something more important to me than pleasing the rest of the parents in our congregation and that was taking every opportunity to prepare my child for the future. I say that for the benefit of you who are in a position in which people constantly watch you and your children.

Anyway, I told Andy to pray about it. Try to imagine the prayer of a tenth grader who is dying to see one of his heroes perform on stage. By his own admission, his prayer sounded something like this, "Dear Lord, You know how much I like ————'s music. You know I don't plan to do anything wrong. So I don't see anything wrong with going to the concert. But if You don't want me to, I won't. So let me know. If I don't hear anything from You, I will take that as an okay."

You can guess what happened; Andy did not hear anything. His mother and I wanted to jump in and forbid him from going. But we did the more difficult thing; we trusted the Lord and prayed for Andy from the time the church dismissed until the time he returned home. I wish I could say that was the end of his concert career, but actually it was only the beginning. From time to time we would bring it up, but always in the context of his conscience and God's will for him. As it turned out, it was more of a phase he was going through than anything else. As we look back now, both his mother and I are glad we handled it the way we did. But it was tough while it was going on—very tough.

If you are going to teach your children that they are ultimately responsible to God, you must back off in order to force them to face their consciences as well as the consequences of their decisions. At times it will be difficult for them, and possibly even embarrassing, but they must learn. Keep in mind that the day will come when they will be on their own. Then they will have no option but to depend upon their relationship with God to guide them morally and ethically. How well they do then will depend to some degree upon the freedom you allow them now and your willingness to work with them through their struggles and failures.

A Modeling Process

Here is the third thing you must do to aid in your children's development in this area: *You must live a life that reflects responsibility to God.* You have a responsibility to model unconditional faithfulness to God. (We will discuss this further in Chapter 11.) Also, you must be careful not to communicate to your children that you think you are getting by with things simply because you don't get caught. Don't brag about talking the police out of a ticket. Don't brag about pulling things over on your boss at work. These things work against you in the long run. The writer of Proverbs said it well:

> The righteous man walks in his integrity;
> His children are blessed after him.
>
> —*Proverb 20:7*

AM I TOO LATE?

As you read this chapter, you may be thinking, *This is all very fine for someone whose son or daughter is still a young child. But what about my teenager who does not feel responsible to me or God or anyone else?* If that is your situation, the approach you take will have to be a little different—and a little more drastic. Explain the basic principle we have discussed here. Tell your young person that the focus of responsibility has to shift as people grow up and enter adulthood. Make it clear that you are turning your teenager over to the Lord and that you plan to leave the disciplining process up to Him.

This may sound extreme. But if your teenager is totally unresponsive to your efforts at discipline, you really have no viable option. I am not suggesting that you ignore your child. I am saying that a teenager who chooses to function as an adult should be treated like one. You have to put your teenager in a position of facing the responsibility that comes with the much-desired freedom, and that involves being directly responsible to God.

When Anna was working with the singles in our church, she did a lot of counseling with young women. Many of them were divorced and had children to support and raise on their own. Being the mother, the daddy, and the breadwinner was often a bigger challenge than these young women felt they could meet.

On one occasion Anna had lunch with a young mother who wanted to discuss a problem with her thirteen-year-old son. As the young woman told her story, Anna quickly saw that the solution to the problem would require an answer from the Lord, not some pat answer. Someone had already suggested that the young mother just "kick the kid out of the house." This advice broke Anna's heart because she knew it could not be in keeping with what God would want to happen.

As the story continued to unfold, Anna's compassionate nature told her that the young woman needed to leave their luncheon with an answer. So Anna began to pray silently and lift it all before the Father. Since the boy was quickly approaching manhood and was the only male in the home with his mother and younger sister, he was beginning to strongly resist his mother's rules and discipline. Although the boy's father was still alive, he had divorced himself from his wife and children and was living in gross immorality. He was certainly not someone who could be relied upon to provide an appropriate model for her son. The mother earnestly wanted to help her son become a responsible young man, but his resistance to her efforts had left her wondering how she could ever accomplish that.

Soon the Father's answer came to Anna in the form of a Scripture that entered her mind: God is a "father of the fatherless" (Psalm 68:5). She proceeded to explain the Scripture to the mother and suggested that the son be given over to God for all of his discipline. The boy had been a Christian for some time, so he had a fairly good understanding of what was expected of him as a follower of Christ. Anna also suggested that her friend pray about doing this, asking God for the right words. Probably the best time to open a discussion about the subject would be when no disciplinary action was needed and when they could be alone and uninterrupted. Anna pointed out that the mother should read the verse to the boy and then explain that the little family would still have rules to live by; however, if the boy failed to obey the rules, he would be disciplined by God rather than his mother.

Several week later, when Anna saw her at church, she was radiant. As she leaned over to hug Anna, she whispered happily, "It worked."

The mother was wise in explaining to her son what she was doing. The Lord then worked in such a way in his heart that he responded positively. If this is the route you feel pressured to take with your son or daughter, rest assured that whom the Lord loves, He disciplines. And the Lord's discipline always has its desired end.

DEVELOPING A LISTENING EAR

One of the benefits of applying the principle discussed in this chapter is that it helps young children understand how to find God's will. It gets children in the habit of looking to the Lord when making decisions. At an early age they are forced to wrestle with discerning God's still small voice from all the other things that crowd their minds. This principle allows children to develop a sensitivity to the impressions of the Holy Spirit. At the same time they learn about God's silence.

A CONCLUDING ILLUSTRATION

A close friend of mine had an interesting experience that serves as a good illustration of this principle. He and his son had been going around and around on the issue of rock music. I do not need to tell you who was on which side. When the boy turned sixteen, my friend called him in for a serious talk. He handed the boy one end of a piece of string while he held on to the other end. He said, "Son, this string represents the issue of rock music. You know my feelings on the subject. You are sixteen now and old enough to decide this issue for yourself. As of today I am setting you free from my expectations in this area. Now it is between you and the Lord." With that, he cut the string, and they cried and hugged.

I admired my friend's courage and creativity. Not only did he give his son freedom while still at home, but he did it in a way that clearly shifted the young man's responsibility from his earthly father to his heavenly Father. We need more creative communication like this in our homes. The more we have, the greater our chances will be of keeping our kids on our team.

APPLYING PRINCIPLE NINE

1. Review the biblical principle in Romans 13:1–7 that serves as the basis for this chapter.

2. Begin to allow your children to prayerfully set their own standards and restrictions in certain areas, preferably those in which the potential consequences are minimal.

3. You must allow your children to follow through with what they believe God has shown them. Think of some ways you can do this.

4. You must demonstrate a life of responsibility to God.

TEN

DISTINGUISHING BETWEEN MORAL AND WISDOM ISSUES

∽

JOHNNY AND LISA WERE HIGH-SCHOOL STUDENTS. After dating for several months, they felt it would be best to stop seeing each other because of a lack of self-control in their physical relationship. One afternoon after he had finished his homework, Johnny thought to himself, *I ought to give Lisa a call.* As he reached for the phone, he felt some hesitancy about calling. *But,* he thought to himself, *there is nothing wrong with calling her.*

When Lisa answered the phone and recognized Johnny's voice, she got excited. They talked for a while and then Johnny said, "Lisa, how about some dinner?" Lisa was thrilled about the prospects of seeing Johnny again. As she began to give her consent, however, she had some hesitation. Then she thought, *There is nothing wrong with just going out to eat.* So she said, "Yes."

After dinner, Johnny thought to himself, *The night is young. Why go home so early?* As he passed their exit on the expressway, there was some question in his mind as to whether or not he had done the right thing. But then he thought, *There's nothing wrong with driving around for a while.*

Before long they were some distance out of town heading down a back road with which Lisa was all too familiar. Something in her wanted to suggest to Johnny that they turn around. *But,* she thought, *there is nothing wrong with driving here.* So on they went.

When they finally pulled off the road into a secluded part of the little park, both had a bad feeling about the whole scene. Yet neither said or did anything to change the direction in which things were headed. Two hours later, as Johnny backed the car onto the road, both sat in silence trying to understand how a perfectly innocent outing could turn into a passionate encounter that left them filled with guilt.

WHERE DID THEY GO WRONG?

As you read the story of Johnny and Lisa, you could probably tell where it was heading. At the same time you could not find fault with their reasoning—or should I say their *rationalizing?* There was in fact nothing wrong with any of

The wise

anticipate trouble,

make every moment count,

and

face the facts.

the things they did right up to their physical involvement. So what was the problem? More importantly, how do we prepare our kids to successfully deal with such situations?

WALKING WISELY

I believe that kids (as well as adults) get themselves into trouble much of the time because the principle of wisdom is ignored. As we will see, this is a principle that is found throughout Scriptures, but even on specific issues about which the Scriptures are silent, the principle of wisdom can help us make appropriate decisions.

Because of a lack of teaching in this area, and because of our evangelical predisposition toward moral absolutes, we sometimes court disaster. We nurture an attitude that says, "If something is not clearly stated to be wrong, then it is okay. And as long as what I am doing is all right, then don't point your finger at me." As a result we may rationalize unwise decisions.

The principle of wisdom is in one sense beyond good and evil. That is, it goes beyond what the Scriptures delineate as right and wrong. Wisdom always takes into account people's past experiences, their weaknesses, and their strengths. The commands of Scripture have universal application, but wisdom's prescriptions are more tailor-made, more individualized. What may be wise for one person may be very unwise for another. This concept will become clearer as we go along.

THE SCRIPTURES AND WISDOM

Many passages in the Old Testament deal with the concept of wisdom. The book of Proverbs is especially concerned with it. Here are some general comments:

> For the LORD gives wisdom;
> From His mouth come knowledge and understanding;
> He stores up sound wisdom for the upright.
>
> *—Proverbs 2:6–7*

> Happy is the man who finds wisdom,
> And the man who gains understanding;
> For her proceeds are better than the profits of silver,
> And her gain than fine gold.
>
> *—Proverbs 3:13–14*

> Keep sound wisdom and discretion;
> So they will be life to your soul
> And grace to your neck.
>
> *—Proverbs 3:21–22*

There are also specific comments that describe traits of people who have wisdom, such as the following:

> The fear of the LORD is the beginning of wisdom,
> And the knowledge of the Holy One is understanding.
>
> *—Proverbs 9:10*

Wise people store up knowledge,
But the mouth of the foolish is near destruction.

—Proverbs 10:14

A wise man fears and departs from evil,
But a fool rages and is self-confident.

—Proverbs 14:16

There are really too many to include here. The book of Proverbs itself is worthy of a study on this subject, but I think you get some idea of what it has to say about wisdom.

One of the best passages dealing with this concept, however, is found in the New Testament. In Ephesians 5:13–14, the apostle Paul exhorted the Ephesian believers to live moral lives. He made it clear to them that they were neither to participate in evil nor to speak of it. On the contrary, he commanded them to expose immoral deeds of evil persons.

He followed this exhortation with a discussion on wise living:

See then that you walk circumspectly, not as fools but as wise, redeeming the time, because the days are evil. Therefore do not be unwise, but understand what the will of the Lord is.

—Ephesians 5:15–17

Before looking at some of the details of the text, we must understand the relationship of these two passages.

Why did Paul turn from a passage dealing with moral absolutes to one dealing with the issue of wisdom?

This question is answered in part by the way verse 15 begins—"See then that you . . ." It communicates the idea of "since this is true, then . . ." The implication is that "if you are really serious about staying morally pure, then you must walk circumspectly." In other words, verses 15 through 17 serve as the guidelines for accomplishing all Paul mentioned in the preceding verses.

Practically speaking, our goal as believers cannot simply be *not to sin.* Rather it must be *to walk wisely* because walking wisely is the means by which moral living is carried out. Wise living provides a safety factor. It is like putting a fence around a pit with a Keep Out sign on it. The fence serves as a means of keeping people out of the pit. As the fence is to the pit, so wisdom is to sin. When followed, wisdom keeps us out of trouble by eliminating the possibility in the first place.

OVERSTATING OUR CASE

This principle is vitally important in child rearing because many of the issues facing our children are not clearly addressed in the Bible. The Bible does not explain whether or not dancing is okay; Paul did not include a chapter on rock music; Jesus never discussed dating; and nobody answered the one question on every teenager's mind, "How far can I go on a date?" I believe such issues must be handled within the context of wisdom. That is, what *does* the

Bible clearly teach? And in light of that, how can we deal with debatable issues in such a way as to remain faithful to what God expects of us?

Unfortunately, we sometimes approach these issues as if the biblical writers addressed them specifically. Out of a desire to protect our children, we overstate our case. Our fear of their potential mistakes causes us to misuse Scripture by making it say what we want it to say. And we sometimes make dogmatic statements that we cannot support. In doing so, we rob our children of opportunities to develop a discerning spirit. Instead of letting them grapple with the tension of what the Scripture clearly teaches and what it does not, we make all their moral and ethical decisions for them, setting up "clear" categories of right and wrong.

A high percentage of the "rebellious" children I have counseled came out of homes where the principle of wisdom was ignored, where almost everything was made into a major moral issue. Everything about which the children expressed an interest was presented as sinful. Anyone they wanted to befriend was viewed with suspicion. Nothing they said was right. And there were always "appropriate" verses to support the parents' side of things. Then the parents wondered why their children had no interest in church and spiritual matters. They wondered why their children would not open up and communicate with them. The answer is simple: Why should children be associated with an institution that, according to the way their parents present it, has no clue about what they are feeling or thinking? Second, why should children bother to communicate their feelings to people who treat them as if they cannot think for themselves?

Ignoring the principle of wisdom has devastating consequences for children when they leave home as well. Once
they enter a nonreligious environment, such as a college
campus, many of the issues that were black and white at
home become gray. All those reasons about why certain
things were to be avoided don't make sense anymore.
Suddenly, teenagers are faced with difficult questions and no
personal convictions to help them cope. They are forced to
make decisions with no training about how to make them.
Why? Because everything was always decided for them.

If this sounds much like what I said in Chapter 9, you
understand perfectly. The principle of wisdom is a principle
that must be taught along with the process of allowing your
children to develop a sense of responsibility to God.

CHARACTERISTICS OF THE WISE

Now let's look more closely at what Paul is saying to us in
Ephesians 5:15–17. There are three things in particular I
think we need to understand from this passage—the wise
anticipate trouble, they make every moment count, and
they face the facts.

Anticipating Trouble

Paul says in verse 15 that the wise "walk circumspectly." The word *circumspectly* conveys the idea of
people proceeding cautiously and carefully examining the
possible consequences of their actions. The wise do not
approach life casually; they live fully aware of Satan's desire

to sneak up on their blind side and destroy them. So, the first characteristic of people who walk wisely is that they *anticipate trouble* in light of past experiences, present weaknesses, and future goals.

I cannot overstress the importance of teaching our children this principle. Christian teenagers rarely plan their first sexual experience. It usually begins with a fairly innocent make-out session that goes too far. Kids do not usually plan to end the evening driving around with a bunch of drunk friends. Teenagers do not set out to blow their minds on drugs. In most of the circumstances that result in our kids getting into trouble, the bottom line is the same: It is not that they plan to get into trouble; it is that *they do not plan not to!* That is why this principle is so important. It teaches our children to anticipate trouble instead of having to react to it. It teaches them to live with a constant awareness of their weaknesses and their negative potential. Thus, this principle helps our children avoid a good deal of temptation.

Making Every Moment Count

A second characteristic of people committed to walking wisely is that they *make every moment count.* Paul says that they walk "not as fools but as wise, redeeming the time, because the days are evil" (Ephesians 5:15–16).

Over the years various other commentators have pointed out how precious time is and how important it is for us to make the most of every moment. We have been told not to squander time, to consider it a gift from God, to treat it as an opportunity, to respect it, and so on. I am sure that we all acknowledge the truth of such statements, but I am equally sure that we don't always act as if we do. The wise especially need to make each moment count for the Lord to counteract the influence of the world.

The wise understand that it takes no effort on their part to be conformed to the world; it is the easiest thing there is. Therefore, the wise take every opportunity to reverse this process; they take every opportunity to renew their minds to the truth in order to counter the constant barrage of lies from the world. Within this context they gain a whole new appreciation for Christian friends and Christian music and Christian activities. At the same time they see a new danger in unchecked exposure to the philosophy of the world, whether through music, friends, movies, or anything else.

Children who are taught to be wise do not approach the questions of what music to listen to, what movies to watch, and what friends to have from the perspective of *what is wrong with them?* They approach these questions from the perspective of *what is the wise thing to do?* In light of past experiences, present weaknesses, goals for the future, and God's desires, they consider what is the best thing to do. And they also think about whether their participation in an activity is the best use they can make of their time.

Facing the Facts

The third characteristic of the wise is that they *face up to what God desires for their lives.* Paul says, "Therefore, do not be unwise, but understand what the will of the Lord is" (Ephesians 5:17). The wise are honest with themselves about what God expects from them. They stop making excuses for sin.

Paul's command to "understand what the will of the Lord is" means to face up to the will of the Lord. In other words, we are not to live as if we don't know what is going on; we are to face up to how certain things affect us; we are to face up to how certain things tempt us; we are to face up to the situations that lead to trouble over and over again.

As we teach our children about how to be wise, we would do well to help them think through how certain things affect their lives. The wise teenager might learn to follow a thought pattern of *if this happens, I should . . .* Here are some examples: If dating a certain person gets me into trouble, I should break up. If going to a certain place to dance puts me in a vulnerable state of mind, I should stop going there. If certain types of music weaken my self-control, I should not listen to them. If being a cheerleader is hurting my walk with God, I should quit the squad.

Paul is saying, "Don't keep playing games with yourself and with God. Don't keep rationalizing what you know is wrong. Be mature. Face your weaknesses squarely and make your decisions accordingly." Don't defend behavior by asking, "What is wrong with this?" Begin asking, "What is the wise thing to do?" And face up to the answer.

EVERYTHING IN ITS PLACE

I hope that by now you can see how the principle of wisdom keeps us from having to put moral labels on every function in society. It keeps us from overstating our point and looking foolish later on. It is easy to make dogmatic statements such as "All rock music is of the devil." But then what do you tell your teenagers when they ask you what is satanic about a song like "Born in the U.S.A." by Bruce Springsteen, a song about Vietnam vets and their struggles after the war? What do you say when they ask you about a song like "Kyrie Eleison" by Mr. Mister, which is a song about life and our need for the Lord's mercy in everyday affairs?

It is easy to tell our children that they should have Christian friends, but how do we balance this with the Lord's command to evangelize the world? How can they win people they do not know? Wisdom and discernment are God's ways of dealing with these difficult questions. Let's look at some practical ways of teaching these things to our children.

Making It Work

The basis of wisdom is truth. If it is *true* that rattlesnakes are poisonous and tend to bite, it is *wise* not to pick one up. If it is *true* that thousands of people are killed in car accidents every year because they were not wearing seat belts, it is *wise* to wear a seat belt. So, to teach wisdom, you must first teach your children the truth. That is, instill in them the clear teachings of Scripture, both its principles and exhortations. Without these, children are not properly equipped to think wisely.

If you don't believe this is true, spend time with lost people. Does the way they reason sound strange? Their presuppositions (the things they view as true) are completely different from yours as a Christian. Therefore, the conclusions they draw about how to live are completely different, yet consistent with their basis of reasoning.

For instance, if there is no God, and if this life is all there is, why stay in an unhappy marriage? If it is true that someone enjoys sex, and if there is nothing beyond this life, is it not smart to have as much sex as possible? I could give example after example of the warped thinking of lost individuals. But it is only warped to us because our basis of thinking is so different and thus our conclusions are different.

If you want your children to draw the right conclusions about life, they must have a clear understanding of what is true and what is not; their understanding of truth must reflect reality. The best way for that to happen is for you to teach them basic Bible doctrines at a young age. I use the term *basic* to emphasize that I am talking about the *clear* teachings of the Scriptures.

Having established what is clear, you then move to the unclear. The second step then is to help your children bridge the gap between the clear instructions in the Bible and the contemporary questions they are struggling with. You move them from the commands of Scripture to the *implications* of those commands for their daily lives. The way to do this is by asking questions—and letting them answer.

For example, let's say Jill comes to her mom all excited about a guy she has met at school. Apparently, this guy has an interest in Jill and plans to ask her out. Mom very casually asks, "Is he a Christian?" Jill looks the other way and says, "I'm not sure. Well, I really do not think so. He never goes to church, and I have heard him criticize a couple of guys who carry their Bibles to school."

Now Mom has a choice to make. She knows that it is not best for Jill to date this guy. She also has the power to prohibit Jill from going out with him. She can put her foot down immediately and say no, supporting her decision by saying something like, "God does not want Christians dating non-Christians." Or she can help Jill decide for herself what is the wise thing to do in light of clear biblical teaching. By handling this as a wisdom issue, Mom can help her daughter develop discernment.

So Mom says, "Jill, do you think you could fall in love with this guy?"

Jill says, "I think I am already in love with him."

"Oh, so you would consider marrying a non-Christian?"

Jill pauses before she asks, "Isn't there a verse or something about that?"

"Yes, there is. Paul said in 2 Corinthians 6:14 that Christians should not be 'unequally yoked' with nonbelievers and that such an arrangement results in all kinds of problems. You know the problems Mrs. Baker has had with her husband; he never wants to go to church; he will not let her attend Bible classes. He has really made life miserable for her. You wouldn't want that kind of marriage, would you, Jill?"

"No," Jill quickly responds.

Mom continues, "Now I know you are talking about a date, not marriage. But you are in the process of developing patterns for dating that you will carry with you the rest of your single life. Who you date will determine in some degree who you fall in love with. Do you see how dating only young Christian men could protect you from getting yourself in a mess later on?"

"Yes," says Jill.

"What do you think is the wise thing to do in this situation?" Mom asks.

I realize that this conversation is idealistic, but I think it gives you some idea about how to use questions to lead children from the clear to the unclear, from moral absolutes to principles of wisdom. This leads us to the third step.

After you have taught your children the truth and have helped them see the wise thing to do in a given situation, you must help them put their decision in the form of a principle. That is, you must help them see the broader implications of the decision. In the situation above, Jill's mother would want Jill to see that this decision applied not only to this one particular guy but also to every guy she meets. Thus, dating only Christians becomes a principle. Since Jill was involved in the decision, she has developed a personal standard, something she can understand and defend, if necessary.

GOD'S WAY

Distinguishing between moral and wisdom issues is certainly an involved way of handling things. I believe, however, it is the biblical way of handling things. It is God's way of helping us handle successfully many of the issues we face as parents. As our culture changes, so will the questions our kids will be forced to deal with. This principle is the key to bringing the clear teachings of Scripture to bear on the unclear areas of our society. If you ignore it, you may find yourself backed into a corner where you are forced to misrepresent God and drive your children away from God, the church, and the family. To incorporate this principle into your thinking and into you family will be one big step in keeping your kids on your team.

APPLYING PRINCIPLE TEN

1. Involve your children in a program so that they can learn the clear teachings of Scripture. This can be through Sunday school, family devotions, Christian school, or any number of things.

2. Help them bridge the gap between the clear teachings of Scripture and the unclear questions of life by asking them questions.

3. Help them put their answers into the form of a principle.

4. Discuss with your children the subject of wisdom. Refer to the Bible verses discussed in this chapter as a starting point. You may want to use a Bible concordance to look up other relevant verses. Can you think of people in the Bible who were considered to be wise? What characteristics of wisdom did they exemplify?

PART FOUR

To keep your children

on your team, you must

KEEP YOUR TESTIMONY

intact

Brethren, join in following my example,
and note those who so walk,
as you have us for a pattern.

—Philippians 3:17

ELEVEN

MODELING UNCONDITIONAL
FAITHFULNESS
TO GOD

᎒

WHENEVER I TALK TO "REBELLIOUS" CHILDREN,
one of my favorite questions to ask is, "How would you
define Christianity?" I have never received the same answer
twice, and rarely do I get what I would consider a correct
answer. The conclusion I have drawn from this is that
Christianity is not what most children rebel against; most of
these children I have talked to do not know enough about
Christianity to know how to rebel against it! No, what they
are rebelling against is "churchianity," an imitation of the
real thing. With this in mind I could best state the thesis of

this chapter in the following way: *If kids are going to reject Christianity, let's make sure they are rejecting the real thing.*

A NO-WIN SITUATION

When parents model a type of Christianity that is full of compromise and contradictions, they put themselves in a no-win situation insofar as keeping their children on their team is concerned. Kids will respond to that kind of situation in one of two ways. Either they will reject Christianity altogether (kids have a low tolerance for hypocrisy), or they will fully embrace the teachings of the Christian faith. In neither case do parents achieve real unity in the family. Half-hearted commitment rarely reproduces itself; it usually polarizes the commitment of those it seeks to influence.

A good illustration of this is what happens every summer around the time for church camp. Let's take one churchgoing family and trace what typically happens. The father makes it to church three Sunday mornings a month and occasionally on Sunday night when something special is going on. He spends the Sunday school hour drinking coffee and socializing. He leaves most of his Christian ethics on the church steps.

For all his inconsistencies, however, he is concerned about the spiritual condition of his son. Freddy is fifteen now and has absolutely no interest in church or spiritual matters. The group he runs around with is anything but wholesome, and his mother suspects he is experimenting with drugs.

But, praise the Lord, it is almost time for church camp, and this year an ex-rock musician is going to give his testimony. Somehow Dad convinces Freddy to go, and sure enough the Lord breaks through and Freddy is wonderfully converted. The following Sunday night Freddy gets up in front of the whole church and surrenders to full-time Christian service. Dad is so "excited" he has to leave the service early to have a smoke. Somehow this is not exactly what he had in mind. *Freddy is taking this Christianity thing a little too seriously. After all, what is going to happen to the family business if Freddy doesn't eventually take over?* thinks Dad.

What happened? Simple, partial commitment to anything is repulsive. Kids, for the most part, are too idealistic to consciously commit themselves to anything halfway. Parents who model partial commitment to Christ put themselves in a no-win situation if their goal is to keep their children on their team.

MAKING THE OPTIONS CLEAR

I have often wondered why so many Christian parents are not making a more significant impact on the moral development of their children. Many such parents ask me, "Where did we go wrong?" When it looks as if a Christian family is really failing, we sometimes want to blame it all on our changing society. But I think it is time we stopped looking at the outside world and take a good look at the inside of our Christian family world.

For many years, I believe, there has been a grave error in our thinking about exactly what makes a home Christian. We need to come to grips with the fact that just because two born-again believers get married, they have not necessarily established a Christian home. We may know that they are two Christians who love each other and have committed themselves to each other in a marriage relationship, but at this point we don't know how much the couple understands about the Christian walk and faith.

When this couple begins a family, several things could happen. Immaturity in the marriage may be a problem because one or both new parents may not have grown up enough to handle the responsibility. In having children, they have to cease being children. This is a difficult adjustment for a lot of young people who get married and have children before they really mature.

Having children before really discussing the subject and reaching an agreement may be a major problem. If a husband and a wife cannot even agree about whether or not to have children, how can they agree about how to raise children in the proper way? I said in Chapter 1 that children should be viewed as gifts from God, but some parents who do not share this attitude convey negative thoughts to their children. This is not the kind of environment that should characterize a Christian home.

I remember when Anna and I decided that we were ready to become parents. We prayed in earnest for God to have His way as to the time this child would be born, and we also left it up to Him about whether the child was to be a boy or a girl. We were delighted to discover not long afterward that a child was on its way. When Andy was born, we were proud parents, and our little country church was also delighted, for he was the first newborn baby in the church for a long time. We had to start a nursery for one, our precious little boy.

Two years passed, and it appeared that Andy would be an only child. But we really did want at least one more (maybe a little girl, please, Lord). So back on our knees we asked again for the Lord to bless us with a child, leaving the details to Him. This time He sent us a beautiful little strawberry blonde bundle of joy we named Rebecca. In Chapter 1 I suggested that you relate to your children the circumstances surrounding their births and childhoods. You can be sure we have told our children many times that they were sent from God as special gifts and a stewardship to us in answer to our prayers.

Regardless of the problems you and your spouse have had to work through so far, one thing is of vital importance if you are to keep the team together: Parents and children need to understand the family's value system. If you, as a parent, do not understand clearly what your value system contains, what it means, and how to communicate it to your offspring, how can you possibly expect them to know it? The *only* way for them to even have a hint is by watching you very closely.

Earl Wilson states this clearly:

Youngsters . . . get more information by observing those persons who are close to them. Children tend to value what they see their parents valuing. If there happens to be consistency between what the parents say they value and what they show, this value will become strong in the life of the child. If there is no consistency, the child will become even more confused. (*You Try Being a Teenager,* 114)

If you plan to keep your children on your team, you have two options: You can either be totally committed or totally uncommitted. Either way there is at least the *possibility* of keeping your children on your team. However, the fact that you are reading this book indicates that there is some sort of commitment on your part. Thus, you really have only one option—total commitment to God and the Christian life.

WHAT IS TOTAL COMMITMENT?

What do I mean by total commitment? I do not mean perfection (for reasons obvious to all of us). What I do mean is *an uncompromising affirmation of God's Word as truth and a diligent, transparent attempt to put it into practice in our moral standards and value system.*

There are four key concepts in this definition that merit attention. First of all is the concept of *an uncompromising affirmation of God's Word as truth.* Volumes have been written on this subject, and it is certainly not my purpose here to write an apologetic for the authenticity of Scripture. Basically, that means you must present God's Word to your children as *the* standard by which life is lived, as God's guideline to successful living. Present God's Word as the authority for both you and your children. They must understand at an early age that even you, their most apparent authority, are under authority. And they must see a demonstration through your actions of your commitment to that authority.

The second concept is implied by the word *diligent*. Children need to see an earnest, energetic effort on your part to do what is right; they must see in you a concern for consistency in what you profess and what you practice. In this way you model for them the correct response to authority. To do otherwise is to undercut your own authority. How can you expect them to respond positively to you as their authority when there are major areas in your life where you ignore God's authority as revealed in His Word?

The third concept is implied in the term *transparent*. Your children must be allowed to see you as a person struggling with temptation, tempers, and the pressures brought about by changing circumstances. It is unfair to hide your struggles from your children in an attempt to present them with some sort of fault-free faith, a faith that has no trials or failures. This brings us to the last concept we want to explore in regard to total commitment.

Your children should be aware to some degree of your failures. For this reason I have included the term *attempt* in my definition. This is not an excuse for sin; it is a matter of coming to grips with reality. Failure is a part of life, and it will be a part of your children's lives as well. They need to learn how to deal with it. Modeling a correct response to failure is part of total commitment.

If you attempt to cover up failure in your walk with God, you plant seeds of doubt in the minds of your children concerning the practicality and reality of your Christian faith. If your children discover your failure on their own, they will have reason to suspect the genuineness of your faith. If your children are never aware of failure on your part and then they fail, they will have reason to doubt the practicality of Christianity for their own lives. We will discuss the concept more in the following chapter.

They Will Remember

Being brought up in an atmosphere of genuine commitment will influence the way children interpret life while at home as well as after they leave. Recently, I was talking to a young single woman in our church who had grown up in a godly home in another city. Upon moving to Atlanta, however, she decided she would experiment with life in the fast lane. As she talked, I was impressed by the fact that her lifestyle was contrary to everything she had been brought up to believe, but her goal was to one day have a family just like the one in which she was raised.

This desire motivated her to clean up her act and restore her broken fellowship with God and the church. She knew that what her parents had was a direct result of their commitment to Christ, and she realized she must make a similar commitment and get her life back on the right track before she could seriously pursue her goal.

This story is not uncommon and serves as more evidence that committed Christian living by parents greatly increases the chances of keeping their children on their team—even if it may sometimes look otherwise. Children from a godly home do not have to look around very long before they see that without Christ there is not much hope for the family.

WHAT ABOUT NOW?

Children do not have to wait until they strike out on their own before the decision-making process is influenced by the precedent set at home. One day I was talking to a college student who mentioned her involvement in a sorority. I asked her about peer pressure, especially in the area of drinking. She smiled and said that though she was kidded at times, all of her friends knew where she stood and they respected her for her conviction not to drink alcoholic beverages. I was really impressed by the ease and confidence with which she expressed her conviction.

As I learned more about her family, I discovered what I believe accounts in part for her unusual security and faith. The year before she started college, the company that employed her father was purchased by a large beer company. He believed that continuing to work for a company linked with an industry that stood for everything he as a Christian opposed was a violation of his conscience. As a result, he was willing to resign after having been with the company twenty years.

With an example like that at home, it is no wonder that

this man's daughter was able to make a stand for what she believed. Over and over again she had seen her parents make the right choices in tough situations, and then she had seen the positive outcome. It was only natural, once she had committed her own life to Christ, to follow suit. Thus, her following their example of faithfulness put her on their team.

A godly example at home will serve as a reminder of God's faithfulness when it is time for children to make tough choices. If children make wrong choices, the consequences that follow will look all the more bleak in light of what they know would have happened had they obeyed because they will have seen from your life the consequences (or should I say rewards) of obedience.

WHAT THEY SEE DETERMINES WHAT YOU GET

What kind of life are you modeling for your children? Do they see Christianity as something you have just tacked onto the rest of your life? Or do they see you striving for all you are worth to be as obedient as you can possibly be? Does your commitment to Christ motivate them to higher commitment? Or do they feel that a higher level of commitment on their part would put a strain on their relationship with you?

Why not give your kids a test? Tell them they have the freedom of saying anything they want and then ask them the questions mentioned in the preceding paragraph. You need to know what you are modeling if you want to keep them on your team. You may need to change what you are modeling to get them on your team to begin with. If the idea of allowing your children to express uncensored feelings about their perceptions of your spiritual condition bothers you, chances are you have been trying to model something both you and your children know is not real. It is time to be transparent; it is time to be real; it is time to get your kids back on your team.

APPLYING PRINCIPLE ELEVEN

1. How would you evaluate your commitment to Christ in light of the definition of total commitment given on page 170?

2. In what part of that definition do you find yourself the weakest?

3. Do you cover your mistakes so your children will not find out about them?

4. If you answered yes to question three, why do you think you cover your mistakes?

5. How do you think your children would respond if you shared your mistakes with them?

6. Arrange a time with the whole family so that your children can have an opportunity to answer the following questions about you as a parent:

- Do you see Christianity as something I have tacked onto my life or as something that is central to everything I do?
- On a scale of one to ten (ten being the highest), how would you rate my commitment to Christ?
- Do you see any habitual inconsistencies?
- Does my Christianity motivate you to higher commitment?
- Does it make you want to abandon the faith altogether?
- When you have a family of your own, in what ways would you want it to be different from this one?
- When you have a family of your own, in what ways would you want it to be similar to this one?
- Will you forgive me for my habitual inconsistencies?
- Will you pray for me as I grow in my relationship with Christ?

TWELVE

ADMITTING WHEN
YOU ARE WRONG

⌘

WHEN WE THINK ABOUT THE IDEA OF MODELING
unconditional faithfulness to God, it is a little overwhelming. We immediately think of our failures and wonder what
the adverse effects of them will be on our children. We all
have times when we communicate a double standard. Such
times are part of being human. So what about our failures?
How do they fit with the goal of being a good role model
and modeling unconditional faithfulness? Do our failures
short-circuit the whole modeling process?

One afternoon I walked into Andy's room to mention
something to him, and I noticed the sun was shining
through his window onto a piece of furniture. Not wanting

the dark colors of the furniture's upholstery to fade, I walked over to the window to close the curtains.

I did not notice, however, that on the floor by the window was his jade chess set. As I walked to the window, I stepped right in the middle of the chess set and sent the pieces flying all over the floor. In my characteristic manner I said, "Andy, you should not put your chess set on the floor; it could get broken that way." Then I walked out of the room.

A few minutes later he walked into my study and leaned against the door. I looked up and asked him what he needed. With a look of concern on his face he said, "Do you realize that you just walked into my room, kicked my chess set all over the floor, scolded me for how I choose to arrange my room, walked out, and never said anything about being sorry for the mess you made?"

Fortunately for me, he was not really mad. In fact we both got tickled as we began to think about what happened. After I apologized, he said something very interesting. He said, "You know, if I had walked in here and confronted you this way and you had defended yourself, I would have really lost respect for you." With that he turned and went back to his room.

I breathed a sigh of relief as I thought of what could have happened to my relationship with Andy over something so trivial as knocking over some chess pieces. Then I thanked the Lord for helping me see my fault and for giving me the courage to apologize.

Nothing builds

communication barriers

faster than

taking away a child's right

to express an opinion

in the home.

THE GREAT COVER-UP

Some parents attempt to hide their mistakes. Usually, they are trying to protect the image they feel responsible to portray—the perfect parents who have their act completely together and who can handle anything at any time. The fact is, however, that we should not be afraid to admit our failures or mistakes to our children. As this example from my own life illustrates, we do more to hurt our reputation with our kids by covering up than by 'fessing up. George Bernard Shaw has stated this truth in this way:

> The best brought-up children are those who have seen their parents as they are. Hypocrisy is not the parents' first duty.

As children grow older, they see through the efforts of their parents to cover up. When this happens, the consequences of covering up a failure outweigh the consequences of blowing it and being discovered. It may be bad to make a mistake, but it is much worse when we are unable to face up to it.

Children do not understand parents' motivation behind their attempts to cover their mistakes. What is communicated to the children is that the parents cannot admit when they are wrong. That may very well be the case, and we will discuss that a little later on. For now, however, we will assume your motivation in covering your mistakes is a sincere desire to be a good role model for your children.

A Greater Consequence—Distrust

When a parent will not admit being wrong, an attitude of general distrust may develop in a child, and that is understandable. To cover up is to lie. It is very difficult for someone to trust another person when that person has lied in the past. The tragedy is that these feelings of distrust usually invade every area of a child's relationship with that particular parent.

I've talked to young men and women in their late teens and early twenties who were still having a difficult time trusting one of their parents as a result of growing up in a home where that parent had never been willing to admit being wrong. Regardless of what their parents said, these kids experienced an immediate feeling of distrust. If allowed to continue, this kind of attitude can destroy the relationship between parent and child, and it can do serious damage to the child's relationship with a spouse later on.

This problem frequently surfaces in marriage counseling. Usually, the wife is having a difficult time trusting her husband. Regardless of how careful he is, regardless of how he acts, he cannot earn his wife's trust. When confronted with the problem of trust in a marriage, I immediately ask the wife, "What was your father like?" Time and time again it turns out that he was untrustworthy when she was growing up. Consequently, she learned early in life to distrust men. Sometimes the husband is unable to trust his wife—or anyone else for that matter—because a parent, usually his father, demanded that everyone in the family agree with his opinions on everything. His word was law in every matter. Of course when the young man became an adult and discovered that his father's opinions weren't 100 percent correct, he did not know what to believe from anyone. These emotions may run so deep and may have become such a part of the personality that it is very difficult for a man or a woman to sort them out and be free. You can see how damaging it can be to try to maintain the superparent image at home. You are affecting not only your children but possibly their children as well.

Communication Breakdown

Another consequence that can result from a parent's unwillingness to admit failure is a communication breakdown. This happens when a child confronts a parent about the parent's error or decision and is then punished for being "disrespectful." Nothing builds communication barriers faster than taking away a child's right to express an opinion in the home. Although this may not be a parent's goal, it may be the only means of keeping the mistake from being exposed. The consequences down the road are devastating.

In counseling teenagers I get them to express their feelings toward their parents. I ask, "If your mom or dad were sitting here and gave you permission to say anything you would like to say, what would you say?"

When they finish, they are often overwhelmed with relief and emotion. Then I say, "Why don't you go home and tell your parents just what you told me."

"Are you kidding? Do you know what my dad would do to me if I talked to him that way?"

"No," I say, "what would he do?"

"He would restrict me forever for talking back like that."

Parents, please do not restrict your kids from expressing their feelings. When you do, you are only cheating yourself. By cutting short their expressions of frustration and even anger, you are cutting short your relationship with them. It is more a reflection of your immaturity than theirs if you are unable to sit through a conversation in which they are critical of you.

They Do What You Do

A third consequence of not owning up to mistakes is that a parent teaches a child to do the same thing. A child needs to know how to deal with failure.

Children naturally take their cue from you. When you cover up your mistakes by deceiving your family or by silencing them, you are in effect saying, "The way to deal with failure is to deny it and to silence those who see things differently." Part of teaching your children how to master life is teaching them how to deal successfully with failure, and this can occur only if you are willing to admit failure in the first place.

Many talented men and women have stopped far short of their potential for accomplishment in life because they failed at some point and were never able to get over it. They never learned to fail successfully. Instead of viewing failure as a challenge, they viewed it as the end of the road. Do your part now so that this cannot be said of your children. Wasted human potential is a great tragedy, and it is certainly not in keeping with what God desires for His children.

BEING THERE

I believe one of the major causes of parents' propensity to cover up mistakes is a misunderstanding concerning the nature of the spiritual life. We tend to have a *product* mentality. That is, we feel pressed to present ourselves, especially to our children, as men and women who have "arrived," men and women who have their act together in every respect—socially, physically, and spiritually.

Of course each of us would be quick to say, "Oh, I have such a long way to go." But let somebody close to us point out a particular element of that "long way" and watch out! We always have an explanation, but the explanation may be no more than a lie: "This is the first time I have ever done that"; "I didn't know"; "I never said that"; "Are you sure that was me?"

If in fact we are responsible for "being there," it is understandable why we would go to great lengths to defend ourselves and to cover up. But whose expectation is that anyway? It is certainly not God's.

Getting There

God does not expect you to be there; He does not expect you to have arrived in any area. In fact He makes it very clear that you will never be all you can be in this life:

> For I consider that the sufferings of this present time are not worthy to be compared with the glory which shall be revealed in us. For the earnest expectation of the creation eagerly waits for the revealing of the sons of God. For the creation was subjected to futility, not willingly, but because of Him who subjected it in hope; because the creation itself also will be delivered from the bondage of corruption into

the glorious liberty of the children of God. For we know that the whole creation groans and labors with birth pangs together until now. Not only that, but we also who have the firstfruits of the Spirit, even we ourselves groan within ourselves, eagerly waiting for the adoption, the redemption of our body. For we were saved in this hope, but hope that is seen is not hope; for why does one still hope for what he sees? But if we hope for what we do not see, we eagerly wait for it with perseverance.

—*Romans 8:18–25*

That being the case, to set as your goal the modeling of a finished product is to set yourself up for failure and fraud.

If anyone could have claimed to be a product of what Christianity was all about, it would have been the apostle Paul. Yet he was quick to say in reference to spiritual maturity, "Not that I have already attained, or am already perfected, but I press on" (Philippians 3:12a).

Paul did not view himself as someone who had arrived. He did not want anyone else viewing him that way, either, even the people he was attempting to lead. But a few verses later he turned around and told them to follow his example:

Brethren, join in following my example, and note those who so walk, as you have us for a pattern.

—*Philippians 3:17*

How can this be?

Paul understood that God was more interested in whether or not he was involved in the *process* of becoming all he could be than whether or not he had *arrived*. He understood that the ultimate question for the concerned Christian was not, Have you arrived? but Are you arriving? Are you involved in the process of becoming conformed to the image of Christ? Are you becoming all God wants you to be?

Paul had no problem asking the Philippian believers to follow his example because he was modeling a process, not a product. Thus, even with his imperfections and his openness about them, he was able with a clear conscience to present himself as their role model.

We have all been tempted at times to fall back on that old saying, Do what I say, not what I do. We all know that does not work in child rearing. Maybe we should change it to say, Seek what I seek, and shoot for what I am shooting for. This is the biblical model for how a leader is to be an example. The same holds true for parents and their children.

The Added Dimension

Probably the best passage on this concept is found in 2 Peter:

> But also for this very reason, giving all diligence, add to your faith virtue, to virtue knowledge, to knowledge self-control, to self-control perseverance, to perseverance godliness, to godliness brotherly kindness, and to brotherly kindness love.
>
> —2 Peter 1:5–7

Peter has painted a picture of a never-ending process, a process in which each facet of the Christian life serves as the basis for another. Yet the perfection of any one facet appears to be a lifetime endeavor. No one could ever claim "perfect" perseverance; the very word suggests continual involvement. The same is true for self-control and diligence. Could God expect a believer to arrive in the area of knowledge? It is unlikely. Again, the implication is that Peter has a *process* in mind.

This becomes even clearer in the verse that follows.

> For if these things are yours and abound, you will be neither barren nor unfruitful in the knowledge of our Lord Jesus Christ.
>
> —2 Peter 1:8

Notice that these qualities are to abound. Like Paul, Peter understood the Christian life to be process oriented and in no way did he let this fact hinder him from acting as shepherd over those God had put in his care. He did not feel pressed to appear perfect in order to lead. He presented himself as one who was seeking to add one facet of the Christian life to the other.

AHHH!

This should come as a great relief to some parents. If you have been living under the burden of thinking that perfect parents modeled perfection, you no doubt have felt somewhat like a failure. Perfect parents, however, seek to model a process. Perfect parents make mistakes, admit them, deal with them in a biblical way, and move on. In so doing, they model the proper attitude toward the Christian life in general, and they provide a biblical model for dealing with failure.

As this principle becomes a permanent part of your thinking, it will affect your whole outlook on life. It will revolutionize your self-esteem as a parent and as a Christian. As with any new concept, however, it takes a great deal of mental renewing for it to sink in.

Next time you make a mistake, do not think of it in terms of your failure as a parent. Do not worry about the adverse effects it may have on your children. Think of it as an opportunity to model God's way of dealing with failure. Turn this negative incident into a learning opportunity for your family.

King David understood this principle of making failure an object lesson for those under his authority. After sinning with Bathsheba, and unsuccessfully trying to cover it up, he wrote:

Create in me a clean heart, O God,
And renew a steadfast spirit within me.
Do not cast me away from Your presence,
And do not take Your Holy Spirit from me.
Restore to me the joy of Your salvation,
And uphold me with Your generous Spirit.
Then I will teach transgressors Your ways,
And sinners shall be converted to you.

—*Psalm 51:10–13*

After publicly admitting his failure, David promised to use what he had learned to teach others. That is good leadership and a good model for parenting.

THAT'S VULNERABILITY!

Still, for many people, admitting to an error will be no easy task, even after coming to grips with the principle outlined here. Something deep inside all of us flares up in defense of our decisions when they are questioned. That "something" is the flesh. Individuals who are walking after the flesh will do anything necessary to keep from looking bad, to keep from looking as if they made a mistake. People who make it a habit of walking after the flesh are, by the very nature of the flesh, insecure. They look only to themselves for a sense of identity and worth, but since the creature has no real significance apart from the Creator, there is a general sense of insecurity. If people look only to themselves for their sense of significance and security, the natural thing to do when confronted about a fault of some kind is to deny it because accusations are direct threats to the security and the sense of self-worth of the individual.

Do you feel threatened when your children question your judgment? Do you find yourself lashing out, overreacting to the situation? Do your children frequently respond, "But all I said was . . ."? You could be suffering from insecurity. On an emotional level, you may feel that admitting error is synonymous with being a failure. This is something you must discover for yourself. But if this pattern is allowed to continue, you will ultimately alienate yourself from your children as well as your spouse.

Don Highlander has this to say about the self-image of a parent:

A positive self image is necessary for parents as well as children. Parents get discouraged, too, and need to learn how to love and encourage each other daily. Instead of defending their "rights" when they make mistakes they need to honestly admit their shortcomings and then attempt to change without reinforcing their frustrations by feeling guilty. Parents who come to grips with the development and nourishment of their personal growth needs can begin to understand how to help a child acquire a positive self concept. (*Positive Parenting*, 164)

What Don says is so true. We as parents must come to grips with our own insecurities and poor self-images if we are to help our children overcome theirs. As long as we are threatened by our children's accusations, as long as we cover up our mistakes, as long as we refuse to face up to our failures, we stifle our own spiritual growth, and we function as stumbling blocks in our children's lives as well.

CAN YOU RELATE?

I heard a story once about a farmer who had some puppies for sale. He made a sign advertising the pups and nailed it to a post on the edge of his yard. As he was nailing the sign to the post, he felt a tug on his overalls. He looked down to see a little boy with a big grin and something in his hand.

"Mister," he said, "I want to buy one of your puppies."

"Well," said the farmer, "these puppies come from fine parents and cost a good deal."

The boy dropped his head for a moment, then looked back up at the farmer and said, "I've got thirty-nine cents. Is that enough to take a look?"

"Sure," said the farmer, and with that he whistled and called out, "Dolly. Here, Dolly." Out from the doghouse and down the ramp ran Dolly followed by four little balls of fur. The little boy's eyes danced with delight.

Then out from the doghouse peeked another little ball; this one noticeably smaller. Down the ramp it slid and began hobbling in an unrewarded attempt to catch up with the others. The pup was clearly the runt of the litter.

The little boy pressed his face to the fence and cried out, "I want that one," pointing to the runt.

The farmer knelt down and said, "Son, you don't want that puppy. He will never be able to run and play with you the way you would like."

With that the boy reached down and slowly pulled up one leg of his trousers. In doing so he revealed a steel brace running down both sides of his leg attaching itself to a specially made shoe. Looking up at the farmer, he said, "You see, sir, I don't run too well myself, and he will need someone who understands."

If you want to keep your kids on your team, you need to let them know you understand; you understand their weaknesses, struggles, and failures; you understand because you have a few yourself. Admit your errors, own up to your mistakes, share your weaknesses, and you will have taken another positive step toward keeping your children on your team.

APPLYING PRINCIPLE TWELVE

1. Begin renewing your mind to the fact that your responsibility as a parent is to model a *process*, not a finished *product*.

2. Begin viewing your failures as opportunities to teach your children how to fail successfully.

3. If you find yourself overreacting when your authority is challenged, take time to think through the possible causes.

THIRTEEN

MODELING YOUR
PROPER ROLE

⌒

THE MOST EXTREME TEENAGE COUNSELING
situations that I have faced as a pastor have come as a direct
result of families violating this principle. When children
grow up in a home where the parents have ignored divinely
assigned roles, they are set up for disaster—morally, emotionally, psychologically, and spiritually. I believe the failure
of parents in this area has caused the rapid growth of the
homosexual community in this country, and I also believe it
is the cause of much of the drug and alcohol abuse among
children and teens. I am not alone in this opinion.
Counselors across the nation are seeing a trend among their
counselees who are suffering from both social and sexual

maladjustments. The same family pattern keeps showing up—*a domineering mother and a passive or absent father.*

Paul D. Meier, M.D., part of a team who heads up a clinic in the Dallas area, says he believes "a domineering, smothering mother and a weak father lie at the root of the vast majority of mental illness in children." After seeing thousands of patients and spending hundreds of hours in research, he concludes that role confusion in the home has the potential for producing homosexuals, sociopathic criminals, schizophrenics, anorexic teenagers, and even hyperactive children (*Christian Child-Rearing and Personality Development,* [Grand Rapids: Baker Books, 1977], 89, 49–78). That is not to say that each one of these cases is the result of improper modeling at home. It is to say, however, that disregarding God's order for the home greatly increases children's chances of suffering one or more of these personality problems.

I believe this so strongly that whenever parents come in for counseling concerning behavioral problems in their children, this is the place I begin my questioning. I sometimes get right to the heart of the problem by asking, "If I asked your son or daughter, 'Who is really in charge at your home?' what do you think their answer would be?"

Time and time again I have seen a mother drop her head and begin to cry as her husband sits silently by and watches. This penetrating question is often the first step to putting a family on the road to recovery, but not always. Many parents run from this question, for it uncovers what many are too proud to admit—a major flaw in the fabric of their homes, a refusal on their parts to assume their God-ordained roles in the home. The result may be denial, and the consequences of such denial are devastating.

FATHER ON THE RUN

I'll never forget one mother who called me about her thirteen-year-old son. She was concerned that he was demonstrating homosexual tendencies. As she described his behavior, I knew she had good cause for concern. After listening for a while, I told her that her son's behavior (especially at his age) was usually a reflection of a deeper problem at home. I went on to tell her that young children with homosexual tendencies characteristically come from homes where the mother is the dominant figure and the father is either absent or passive. There was a pause. And then tears.

She admitted that there was a serious role problem in their home. I suggested that she and her husband should come in for a counseling session. The morning of the appointment, however, a man called and canceled. I imagine it was her husband. I never heard from them again, but I can almost guess what happened.

There is something very threatening to a man when he has to face up to the truth about neglecting his role at home. I imagine that when the father of this home heard from his wife how I diagnosed the problem, he decided not to come. Usually, a father in that situation wants to believe that his *child* has the problem, not *him*. The very thought of being to blame for a son's homosexual tendencies is more than many men can bear. Consequently, they run, and the problem is never handled.

195

It is not

what you think

that influences

your children,

it is what you

communicate.

FATHER ON A LEASH

A scene that is all too common to me is Mom leading Dad down the aisle of the sanctuary after the service to talk to me about their wayward child. Usually, the conversation becomes a monologue as Mom pours out her heart and Dad stands by, nodding now and then in agreement. The blame is often placed on some neighbor child who has been a bad influence on their child. Sometimes a bad school system receives the blame. On and on she goes. She assures me that if I could take an hour out of my busy schedule to talk to their child, she is sure everything would be fine.

But I know better. I know that ten hours of counseling with their child would do no good unless Mom and Dad are willing to make some changes. I know that an hour of counseling can be undone in five minutes of family interaction when the roles are confused. And the worst thing of all is that I know unless Dad is willing to get involved in the process, there is little hope for change.

WHY ALL THE CONFUSION?

The preceding discussion raises two important questions: (1) Why is there such a tendency on the part of husbands to sit back and let their wives dominate the family? and (2) Why is there such a tendency on the part of wives to take control? To answer these questions, we need to look all the way back to the first husband-and-wife relationship.

When God made the first man and woman and put

them in the Garden of Eden, they functioned together in perfect unity. What he needed she provided, and what she needed he provided. This is implied by the inclusion of the phrase "a helper comparable to him" in Genesis 2:18 and then again in verse 20. Literally translated this phrase says, "I [God] will make him [Adam] a *corresponding helper*" (Genesis 2:18b) (Allen P. Ross, *The Bible Knowledge Commentary,* [Wheaton, Ill.: Victor Books, 1983], 31). The picture painted for us is that both the man and the woman were completely satisfied as they functioned in their God-ordained roles. Thus, there was no conflict.

After they sinned, however, a change took place not only in their relationship with God but also in their relationship with each other. The result of this change was acted out when God approached Adam and Eve in the Garden. Alienation replaced unity. Adam was quick to turn on Eve when confronted about his disobedience.

God pronounced judgment on all the parties involved, beginning with the serpent:

> Because you have done this,
> You are cursed more than all cattle, . . .
> On your belly you shall go . . .
> And I will put enmity
> Between you and the woman,
> And between your seed and her Seed.
>
> —*Genesis 3:14–15*

From the serpent God moved to Eve:

> I will greatly multiply
> your sorrow and your conception;
> In pain you shall bring forth children;
> Your desire shall be for your husband,
> And he shall rule over you.
>
> —*Genesis 3:16*

I believe verse 16 provides the explanation about why there is a power struggle in many homes today. To get the full impact of this verse, we need to understand the context as well as the author's use of the word *desire*.

The context of this verse is that of judgment. The things pronounced by God did not come as good news to those involved. It was not good news to the serpent that he would be cursed more than any other animal. Nor was it good news that he would have to crawl from then on. It was not good news to Adam that he would have to work the rest of his life; instead of picking fruit provided by God, he would have to grow it himself (see Genesis 3:17–19). Along the same lines, it was not good news to Eve that she would have to suffer in childbirth, and that "cheery" bit of information was followed by two key phrases:

> Your desire shall be for your husband
> And he shall rule over you.

The context seems to indicate that this was bad news too. That is, the idea of Adam's ruling over her was clearly viewed as punishment like everything else God had mentioned to that point.

Another clue here supports the idea that this whole passage carries with it a negative tone is the term *desire*. This term appears again in the narrative of Cain and Abel. There we get a clearer idea of its full meaning.

After Cain realized that God was not pleased with his offering, God said to him,

> Why are you angry? And why has your countenance fallen? If you do well, will you not be accepted? And if you do not do well, sin lies at the door. And its *desire* is for you, but you should rule over it.
> —*Genesis 4:6–7, emphasis added*

The latter part of verse 7 is about a struggle for control. Sin, as personified by the author, was struggling for control over Cain, but Cain was expected to overcome sin and "rule over it," or master it. The author used the term *desire* to communicate the idea of mastery or control. I believe the idea of mastery is what the author had in mind when he used the term *desire* in relation to God's pronouncement of judgment on Eve. That is, part of her judgment was that she would naturally desire to master her husband, but he would in fact be expected to rule over her. Thus, from the very beginning there was built-in potential for a power struggle between a husband and a wife. This certainly came as bad news to Eve.

And the Curse Goes On

There is no denying that the curses related to the serpent and to Adam are still in effect today. Anybody who has ever planted a garden knows that. Therefore, it is not unreasonable to assume that the curses related to Eve are still in effect as well. Any woman who has had a baby knows from experience that this is the case. However, I think many men and women have a tendency to overlook the implications of verse 16.

If I have interpreted it correctly, it means that every woman has a certain negative potential that is as real as the pains of childbirth. I believe that as a result of the Fall there is within every wife a natural resistance to the authority of her husband. This is certainly more obviously expressed in some cases than in others. And it has a great deal to do with how well the husband is fulfilling his responsibilities at home, responsibilities he will have a tendency to neglect since he, too, is cursed.

I am not saying that every wife is consciously trying to control her husband. I am saying that every wife has the potential and needs to be aware of it. I am also saying that when this potential goes unchecked in a woman who is married to a man neglecting his God-given responsibilities, the roles naturally become confused and can get reversed. The result is a domineering wife and a passive husband. The trend we see toward role reversal in our society is simply the playing out of the original curse. Unfortunately, children who come out of these types of homes often suffer the greatest consequences, and it is for their sake that I have gone into such great detail here.

GETTING TO THE BOTTOM OF THINGS

The apostle Paul was certainly aware of the tendency of husbands and wives to confuse their roles. Why else would he begin with the issue of submission when addressing wives in his epistles? Why else would he begin with the issue of love when addressing husbands?

> Wives, submit to your own husbands, as to the Lord. For the husband is head of the wife, as also Christ is the head of the church.
>
> *—Ephesians 5:22–23a*

> Husbands, love your wives, just as Christ also loved the church and gave Himself for her.
>
> *—Ephesians 5:25*

> Wives, submit to your own husbands, as is fitting in the Lord. Husbands, love your wives, and do not be bitter toward them.
>
> *—Colossians 3:18–19*

The Colossians passage is especially interesting in that these two verses are the total of Paul's advice in this epistle to husbands and wives regarding their relationship with each other. Paul knew that the issues of love and submission were really the bottom line. He understood that the tensions that arise in a marriage are usually associated with an abuse of one or both of these maxims. When a husband loves his wife the way he should and his wife submits to him as the head of the home, everything else seems to fall into place. That being the case, Paul went right to the heart of the matter in his discussion (or should I say his mention) of the marriage relationship.

Submission

The idea of submitting to someone usually conjures up negative images in our minds. We tend to think of people bowing and scraping, of slaves, and of all-around abuse, both mentally and physically. But that is not the picture given in Scripture. God set forth the concept of submission in the context of a loving, sacrificial relationship. Only when we isolate the concept of submission do negative images appear. It is then that we think about all the awful things we have seen take place in marriages where a wife tried to submit and suffered for it. In its proper context, however, submission is the logical response of a wife to a husband.

I will never forget a conversation I had one afternoon with a woman journalist. She was raking me over the coals about a Mother's Day sermon she heard me preach. In this sermon I had stressed the responsibility of wives to submit to their husbands. This journalist proceeded to tell me that this submission stuff was "trash" and that if I thought she was going to be a "doormat" for some guy to wipe his feet on, I was crazy.

I assured her that I was not suggesting anything like that. Then I asked her to imagine something with me. I said to her, "Imagine being married to a man who loved you with all his heart. A man who cherished you, took care of you, always placed you before himself. Imagine a man who was sensitive, yet strong. A man who made you proud to be with him."

On and on I went, describing what I think God wants every husband to be for his wife. As I talked, I literally saw this woman's countenance change. The harshness faded. The criticism left her eyes. When I finished, I said, "Now, do you think you would have any trouble submitting to a man like that?"

"With pleasure," she said.

This young woman was suffering from what many people suffer when it comes to the idea of submission—an unbalanced perspective.

Submitting to an Unloving Spouse

If every husband was like the one I just described, there would be no need for this chapter or for this book, for that matter. Submission is usually not a major issue in a home unless a husband neglects his role or a woman has grown up in a home where her father neglected his role and her mother struggled with submission, leaving her daughter a poor example. In both cases, however, a man's refusal to fulfill his role was part of the problem.

In the case of an unloving husband, a wife still has a responsibility to be submissive. Peter made this clear when he wrote,

> Wives, likewise, be submissive to your own husbands, that even if some do not obey the word, they, without a word, may be won by the conduct of their wives, when they observe your chaste conduct accompanied by fear.
>
> —1 Peter 3:1–2

I am totally aware of the difficulty in applying this principle. A friend, whom I will call Ray, told me his story. His father died when he was a baby. His mother remarried when he was eleven, and the man she married turned out to be a totally irresponsible human being. He abused him and his mother until Ray was old enough to become a threat to his stepfather physically. Through all of that, however, his mother continued to serve and submit to her husband. Recently, Ray asked her why she put up with what she did those many years. She looked at him as if he had said something disrespectful. Then she answered, "When I married him, I promised to love him for better or for worse."

It is difficult for me to comprehend that kind of love. But as I look around at the children that come out of homes where Mom refuses to fulfill her God-given role, I wonder what would have happened to Ray if his mother had used his stepfather's responsibility as an excuse to leave? Mom, I know it can be tough. But for the sake of your children, submit to your husband. Your obedience in this matter may be their only hope for a healthy childhood.

Anytime there is a threat of physical abuse from a husband, I do not hesitate to recommend separation for a time. But I would never recommend that a wife take over the household while her husband is still at home. To do so is to assume a role God never intended for her to fulfill. (For an excellent discussion on submission to unloving husbands, see Darien B. Cooper's book, *We Became Wives of Happy Husbands*.)

Loving a Wife

Although the biblical authors usually addressed the wife first in their discussions on marriage, most of what was said was directed to the husband. There seemed to be little need for an explanation of what it meant to submit to one's husband.

However, the idea of loving one's wife needed both explanations and illustrations. The importance of the wife's role was not minimized, but the difference in emphasis may have had something to do with the magnitude of the husband's responsibility.

When the apostle Paul exhorts husbands to love their wives, he certainly has more in mind than a kiss on the cheek on the way out the door each morning. The illustration he chooses makes this painfully clear:

> For the husband is head of the wife, as also Christ is head of the church; and He is the Savior of the body. Therefore, just as the church is subject to Christ, so let the wives be to their own husbands in everything. Husbands, love your wives, just as Christ also loved the church and gave Himself for her, that He might sanctify and cleanse her with the washing of water by the word, that He might present her to Himself a glorious church, not having spot or wrinkle or any such thing, but that it should be holy and without blemish. So husbands ought to love their own wives as their own bodies; he who loves his wife loves himself. For no one ever hated his own flesh, but nourishes and cherishes it, just as the Lord does the church. For we are members of His body, of His flesh and of His bones.
>
> —*Ephesians 5:23–30*

Paul compares the love a husband is to have for his wife to the love Christ has for the church. If that is a fair comparison, a husband has an incredible task ahead of him. He must be the provider, protector, servant, intercessor, motivator, and decision maker. All this and more is associated with the term *love* in the context in which Paul uses it.

There is no allowance for passivity and laziness on the part of the husband. There is no allowance for self-centeredness, either. Christ gave His life for the church. In the same way a husband is to be willing to give his life for his wife. Husband, you are responsible for fulfilling this role in your home. To fail to do so is to pressure your wife into a role God does not intend for her to fill as long as the two of you are together. Second, to ignore your God-ordained role is to set children up for temptations they otherwise could avoid.

A STARVING GENERATION

It grieves me deeply to see children bear the consequences of a father's refusal to take seriously his role in the home. When a father ignores his role, his children starve for the male affection they need to mature both sexually and psychologically. The result is that children from these homes are driven to make up for this lack of male affection in other ways.

Girls from homes where Dad failed to fulfill his role may make up for his affection by finding it through relationships with men. Girls from homes like this are easy prey for guys, especially older ones, with the wrong intentions. Their eyes seem to say, "Take me. I'm available." Since they have never experienced real love from a male, it is almost impossible for them to distinguish between that and lust. Time and time again they will fall in with the wrong type of guy until they get into serious trouble. Anyone who has worked in a crisis pregnancy center knows about the high percentage of girls who have a background similar to the one described here.

I will never forget a fourteen-year-old in our church whose dad basically ignored her for the first few years of her life and then finally left home. Whenever our youth group would go anywhere, she would almost always end up meeting some undesirable guys.

After observing this pattern in her for some time, I decided to say something. I pulled her aside after a service one evening and said, "I know this may sound strange, and I hope you are not offended, but I have seen a pattern in you that really concerns me."

She was shocked, to say the least, but she told me to continue.

I said, "I have noticed that guys are very attracted to you. What really concerns me, though, is the type of guy I often see you with." I went on and explained my fear for her and her need to be discerning in that particular area of her life.

Several weeks later she excitedly told me that she had a new boyfriend and that she could hardly wait for me to meet him. She told me how great his family was and how cute he was and that he had even agreed to come with her to church. I smiled and encouraged her to bring him.

The following Wednesday night my heart sank when I met him. He seemed no different from the guys she usually went with. He looked the other way when I reached out to shake his hand. He did not have much to say and only muttered responses to my questions. All the time, however, the young girl was just glowing with pride.

Less than a month later I was sitting in my office with her

and her mother, both of them in tears. The young man had pressured her into having sex with him, and for reasons unknown to her, she had given in. "I don't know why I said yes," she said, wiping the tears from her cheeks. "I did not even enjoy it."

I can remember how angry I was that night. Not with the young girl, although she was certainly responsible for her actions. I was angry with her father, even though I had never met him. You see, by abandoning his family, he set his daughter up for what eventually happened. He was too selfish to give her the love and affection she so desperately needed as a young girl growing up. He was too self-centered to make the personal sacrifices necessary to guarantee her a fair chance at growing up sexually and psychologically healthy.

Dad, if you are man enough to bring a little girl into this world, for her sake you better be man enough to assume your role of leadership in the home and provide for her the love and affection she needs. And the same thing can be said about what you should provide for your son. Simply providing for your children financially and educationally is not enough. You owe them a debt of love. If you fail to do that, you set them up for disaster.

THE SAME OLD STORY

I have already mentioned that I believe the growth of the homosexual community is greatly due to a refusal on the part of parents to fulfill their proper roles in the home. I have yet to counsel with a man or a woman who was practicing homosexuality whose parents assumed proper biblical roles in the home. In fact, a friend who often counsels with persons practicing homosexuality told me that when his counselees begin telling him about their background, he often stops them in the middle of the story and finishes it for them! He has heard the same story so many times that he knows what comes next.

Without fail, one or both parents refused to assume biblical roles in the home. As a result, their son did not get the affection he needed from his father and thus grew up with a deficiency. Unaware of the real problem, such young men seek to make up for what they missed through sexual relations with other men.

Don't get me wrong. These men are totally responsible for their behavior. One day they will give an account to God for it. But they are not the only ones who will have to give an account. Their parents are responsible to some degree. Homosexuality is not an inherited disorder. It is a learned behavior rising out of a deep need for affection from the parent of the same sex, which is a need that should have been met at home. Dr. Paul Meier says, "It [homosexuality] will be more of a temptation for those who have not had a strong parent of the same sex to identify with, especially during the first six to ten years of life" (*Christian Child-Rearing and Personality Development*, 55).

COUNTING THE COST

Dad, passing off your lack of leadership in the home by kidding about how much more capable your wife is may be good for a laugh with the neighbors, but it is no laughing matter in view of the effects it could have on your children. Mom, running the home because Dad is constantly forgetting to do things or because you are so much more capable may get the bills paid on time, but you may lose your son in the meantime.

God did not assign us roles just to give us something to do. His assignments were made with our children in mind. A submissive wife and a loving husband provide a solid basis for the mental and sexual health of children.

You can drag your children to church every time the doors are open. You can read the Bible to them every night of their lives. You can send them to all the church camps. But, Dad, if you are not loving and leading your wife, and, Mom, if you are not graciously submitting to your husband, more harm is being done than good.

I've met preachers' sons who were practicing homosexuals, and they could quote the Bible backward and forward. I've done crisis pregnancy counseling with churchgoing Christians' daughters who had all the "right" biblical answers, but for all the Bible they knew and for all the wisdom they had, they felt driven on the inside to find the love they never received at home. On the other hand, some of the finest, most balanced, and well-adjusted men and women I have met in my life have come from homes where neither parent was a believer, but Dad adored Mom and Mom submitted to and willingly served Dad.

The point is simply this: God gave each of us a role to fulfill in the home. Dad, you are to love your wife as Christ loved the church. Mom, you are to submit to your husband.

To ignore these principles, regardless of what else you do to try to compensate for them, is to set your children up for failure. On the other hand, fulfilling your God-ordained role in the home is taking a giant step toward keeping your children on your team.

APPLYING PRINCIPLE THIRTEEN

1. Ask your children who they think controls your home.

2. Study the following passages and ask God to give you insight into how you can better fulfill your role in the home: Ephesians 5:22–23; Colossians 3:18–21; 1 Peter 3:1–7.

3. Wife, ask your husband if he thinks you have a submissive spirit—not simply if you *act* submissive, but if you communicate a spirit of submission.

4. Husband, ask your wife if she feels confident that you are in control of things at home or if she feels the burden of the home is on her shoulders.

AFTERWORD

⁊

I FELT I COULD NOT CLOSE THIS BOOK WITHOUT offering you a few more words of encouragement. We have discussed various ways that can help you keep your kids on your team, and I know that a lot of time, effort, faith, and prayer will have to be involved if you are to accomplish that goal. But I have confidence that you are willing to go the extra mile (or more).

Your desire to pursue the subject is a really positive step toward beginning to think correctly, treat your children correctly, teach them correctly, and present a testimony that is intact—all the things that are part of getting your kids on your team and keeping them there. I was able to raise my two children in this way, and now that they are responsible young adults, I know that it was all worth it. As you can tell from personal examples I have given, it has not always been easy. Like all parents, I have had to struggle at times.

Children deserve all the assistance we can give them as we prepare them to enter the world on their own. They will have enough to contend with in that rather hostile environment without having to overcome serious problems that are a result of our failure to fulfill our parental obligations to them according to God's instructions.

Just as the Father loves us, so we are to love our children; we are to *communicate* unconditional love and acceptance. Please note that emphasis on the word *communicate*. It is what we communicate to our children that is important. We must guide them through their young lives as they learn that their true identity is to be found in who they are in Christ, and we must teach them to become adults submitted to God's authority, responsible only to Him.

I hope you have taken advantage of the applications of the principles found at the end of each chapter. Reading about these principles is only the first step; implementing them is the second.

My prayers go with you as you undertake to keep your kids on your team. Do not be discouraged because it may take longer than you think it should to implement each principle. Just keep remembering whose team you are on and call on the Leader of that team at any time, in any situation. He is always there for you, and He is certainly supportive of what you are trying to accomplish. So, take heart and begin!

STUDY AND
DISCUSSION GUIDE

❦

APPLYING THE PRINCIPLES OF THIS BOOK TO your own life, and to the lives of your kids, will be easier if you invest the time to complete the study and discussion guide on the following pages. This guide will challenge you to be realistic in reviewing your perspective about your kids and your spouse. It has been designed to stimulate your thinking and encourage you to take actions that help build a strong and loving parent-child relationship.

Have a pencil and some paper on hand. Now get started!

CHAPTER 1:
VIEWING YOUR CHILDREN
AS GIFTS FROM GOD

1. Compare your attitude about your children's place in your home with the idea expressed in Psalm 127:3.
2. How would you describe the manner in which you usually communicate what you are thinking to your kids?
3. As a Christian, what sort of standards do you invoke to determine the value of your child?
4. How do you think your children perceive their places in your life?
5. List at least three ways you communicate to your children how they play a positive role in your life.

CHAPTER 2:
VIEWING YOUR CHILDREN
AS A STEWARDSHIP FROM GOD

1. To whom are you responsible for the keeping of your children?
2. If you are not already doing so, plan a little time each day to talk with your kids about something of God. List some topics that are appropriate to the ages of your children.
3. How would you describe, in general, a good approach to answering your kids' questions?
4. What does it mean to "let go and let God" with your kids?
5. Do your kids understand your responsibility to them as a parent, according to the Scriptures? If you have never talked to them about this, try to arrange a suitable moment to explain it to them. Note some ideas to include in your explanation.

CHAPTER 3:
DEMONSTRATING AN INTEREST
IN THEIR CHILDHOOD EXPERIENCES

1. Try to list the actual time, in hours and minutes, you have spent with your kids in the last seven days. Just being in the same house doesn't count!
2. When was your last family powwow? How does that relate to the last event involving the whole family, such as a major purchase or a trip?
3. When one of your kids asks for help in making a decision, do you view the situation from his or her perspective or from your own? In what ways can you better view the situation from the child's perspective?
4. If you asked your kids what kind of listener you are, what do you think they would say?
5. After your kids have finished telling you something, how do you respond? Do you comment about it, or do you quickly change the subject to something you consider more interesting?
6. Be aware that when you pay little or no attention to the child's remarks, the child will take that as a lack of interest in him or her as a person. What responses can you make to convey interest in your child?

CHAPTER 4:
LOVING AND ACCEPTING YOUR CHILDREN UNCONDITIONALLY

1. If you are not satisfied with your performance, does it affect your acceptance of your children's performance? If you answered yes, how does your behavior reflect that attitude?

2. What does unconditional love for your children mean to you?

3. Do you frequently compare the performance of one child in the family to another? What is the likely outcome of this tactic?

4. Can you relate rebellious feelings or behavior in your youth to your kids' behavior? What have you learned about that behavior?

5. Are most conversations with your kids task or performance oriented, or are they character oriented? How do you recognize the difference between the two?

6. Set aside a time and plan a strategy to implement the four suggestions to overcome *conditional acceptance* of your children. Begin by rereading pages 55–56.

7. Examine your life to see if personal insecurity hampers your ability to love your kids. If so, what are you willing to do to overcome that insecurity?

CHAPTER 5:
SETTING LOVING LIMITATIONS

1. Have you established reasonable limits for your children's behavior (courtesy, respect, self-control)? What could be the result of failing to do so?
2. Write down your strategy for setting limits for your children's behavior. If you don't have a strategy, formulate one now. (See the four principles starting on page 63.)
3. What is the consequence of not explaining to your children your reason(s) for not permitting something?
4. How can you clearly communicate the consequences of disobedience? (Imagine one or two possible examples of disobedience, and script specific responses you can use. Think in terms of a role-playing approach.)
5. In what ways can you allow your kids to participate in setting the consequences (punishment) for their misbehavior?
6. List the rewards you give your kids for their positive behavior. Can you list at least five?
7. Do you think there is a proper age to begin the discipline of a child? If the answer is yes, what is the proper age? Is it the same for each of your children?
8. You need to have a common objective for any rules you set up for your kids to ensure consistency in the application of discipline. What is the common objective of the rules for your kids in your house?

CHAPTER 6:
HANDING DOWN YOUR FAITH

1. Spiritually speaking, what are you going to leave behind for your kids when you die?

2. If you have never written down the spiritual truths that guide your life, do so now. If your children are not old enough to understand, put your writing in an envelope to be given to them later.

3. When was the last time you praised each child?

4. Ask your children to identify spiritual truths that have helped them through a difficult time in their lives. Note their responses. (You may want to remind them of their responses at a later time in their lives. How have they grown spiritually?)

5. Relate to your kids an experience in your life, when you were about their age, that helped you mature spiritually. It may be a story by a parent or grandparent, something you observed, or something you were involved in directly.

6. What do you think is the best way to demonstrate the importance of prayer to your children?

CHAPTER 7:
PROVIDING FOR YOUR CHILDREN

1. What does the Bible say about Christians who fail to provide for their families?
2. What, if any, do you think are the limits on being a good provider?
3. Describe the difference between a *want* and a *need*.
4. Have you ever, perhaps subconsciously, related love to the number of things you could provide? What were the circumstances?
5. We must fulfill three emotional needs for our children: *a sense of belonging, a sense of worthiness,* and *a sense of competence.* List two things you do in each of these areas to fulfill the emotional needs of your children. (See pages 110–114.)
6. Have you accepted Jesus Christ as your personal Savior? If not, how have you been providing for your children's spiritual needs?
7. God has sent the Holy Spirit to provide for the earthly needs of His children. Discuss with the whole family how God has provided for all family members, each in his or her own way.

CHAPTER 8:
TEACHING YOUR CHILDREN
THE IMPORTANCE OF PRAYER

1. If one of your children asked, "What is prayer for?" what would your answer be?
2. How do you regularly encourage your kids to pray about the decisions they must make in their lives? How do they see you doing this in your life?
3. Organize a family prayer session, perhaps weekly for fifteen or twenty minutes. Invite every family member to participate by sharing needs and concerns and by praying.
4. In what ways can you encourage your children to talk with God in their own way during their quiet time?

CHAPTER 9:
TEACHING YOUR CHILDREN TO WHOM THEY ARE ULTIMATELY RESPONSIBLE

1. Read and discuss Romans 14:10–12 with your kids. You may want to make some notes to yourself about points to raise.
2. What does it mean to transfer your children's feelings of responsibility from Mom and Dad to God?
3. What could be the consequences of waiting until your kids are "old enough" to understand the meaning of responsibility?
4. You should *sell and not tell* your kids about using God's values to set standards in their lives. What are some ways you can do this?
5. Ask your kids to whom they feel responsible and why. Don't limit it to Mom and Dad.
6. Are you prepared to sit back and wait for your kids to implement what God has shown them? If the answer is no, what steps can you take to change the answer to yes?
7. How are you demonstrating before your children a lifestyle that reflects your responsibility to God?
8. Hold a family discussion time and use Psalm 68:5 as the subject.
9. How can you use creative communication to make a point with your kids? (Read the illustration on pages 144–145 for one idea.)

CHAPTER 10:
DISTINGUISHING BETWEEN
MORAL AND WISDOM ISSUES

1. Reread with your kids the story of Johnny and Lisa on pages 146–147. Discuss with them what was wrong with Johnny's and Lisa's thinking.
2. If something is not absolutely stated to be wrong in the Scriptures, then it must be okay. Do you agree or disagree with this statement? Can you think of examples?
3. In your opinion, is it, or is it not, right to expose the immoral deeds of evil persons? Why, or why not?
4. Can you back up statements about moral behavior with Bible references?
5. If you want your children to draw the right conclusions about life, of what must they have a clear understanding?
6. Try to engage your kids every day in a brief discussion of their activities. Don't overdo it!
7. Do you involve your kids in establishing their moral guidelines rather than dictating yours? If the answer is yes, how do you do it?
8. Prepare a list of Scripture references to answer your kids' questions about moral issues that may not be clear to them. You may include references to lying, respect, decision making, and sexual conduct (depending on their ages).

CHAPTER 11:
MODELING UNCONDITIONAL FAITHFULNESS TO GOD

1. Ask your kids to explain Christianity. Ask what they think of it.
2. What makes a house a Christian home? List at least five things.
3. Do you, your spouse, and your kids understand how the family's value system works? If the answer is no, what steps can you take to clarify the system?
4. Are you trying to practice a *fault-free faith*? You should be sharing with your children, to the extent that it is appropriate, that as an adult you also have problems. When was the last time you brought the kids up to date on a problem that was mostly a parental one, but its resolution could affect the entire family?
5. Discuss with your children how trying to live by Christian principles could put a strain in their lives. Talk about how to ease that strain.

CHAPTER 12:
ADMITTING WHEN YOU ARE WRONG

1. The typical adult tendency is to cover up our mistakes. Children don't understand that. Ask your kids how adults they know try to hide their errors. Don't let Mom and Dad take all the heat. They must know some other adults!

2. How do you react when your opinion or your statement is challenged by one of your children? Can you explain your reactions in a nondefensive manner?

3. Think about how you could have turned your last mistake into an opportunity to model God's way of dealing with children. How can you turn that negative incident into a positive opportunity for interacting with your children in the future?

4. Do you and your spouse encourage and nurture each other, emotionally and spiritually, to maintain a positive parental self-image? Talk to each other about how you accomplish this.

5. To let your kids know you understand their struggles, you need to show three things. Memorize them, and try hard to put them into practice. (See page 191.)

CHAPTER 13:
MODELING YOUR
PROPER ROLE

1. What are God's roles for husband and wife? Read pages 201–207 with your spouse. Talk about each other's present role in the family, and compare it to God's plan for the family. Can you identify any behavior changes that need to be made?

2. Do you agree that nearly every woman has a negative potential, that is, a natural resistance toward the authority of her husband? (See page 201.)

3. How do you see the idea of a wife's submission in its biblical context?

4. Read and discuss Ephesians 5:23–30 with your spouse. Observe the emphasis on the husband's role.

5. Why do you think God assigned us our roles as husband and wife? What purpose have these roles served and what is their purpose in modern times?

6. The key to keeping your kids on your team is *communication*. Out of the many suggestions in this book, perhaps only a handful are needed to strengthen your position as a loving and concerned parent. Write these suggestions on paper now, keep the list near, refer to it often, and act on it!

ACKNOWLEDGMENTS

I am grateful to my son, Andy, for his invaluable help in compiling and editing the contents of this book. I am also grateful to Victor Oliver for his encouragement and editorial assistance.

About the Author

DR. CHARLES F. STANLEY IS FOUNDER AND president of In Touch Ministries, whose *In Touch* radio and television ministry is broadcast around the world in thirty-five languages. He has also been the senior pastor of the 15,000-member First Baptist Church in Atlanta, Georgia, for more than thirty years.

Dr. Stanley received his bachelor of arts degree from the University of Richmond, his bachelor of divinity degree from Southwestern Theological Seminary, and his master's and doctor's degrees from Luther Rice Seminary. He has twice been elected president of the Southern Baptist Convention and is the author of many books, including *God Is in Control, Seeking His Face, Walking Wisely, The Source of My Strength, Success God's Way,* and *How to Listen to God.*

FINDING PEACE

GOD'S PROMISE OF A LIFE FREE FROM REGRET, ANXIETY, AND FEAR

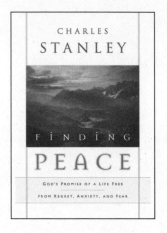

In times of crisis and confusion, Dr. Charles Stanley has learned the one phrase that can carry him through: "God, You are in control." The peace he has experienced in life stems from that foundational belief. In *Finding Peace*, Dr. Stanley shares with readers how they, too, can experience an unshakeable peace which "passes all understanding."

Filled with encouragement to lift the soul, *Finding Peace* offers insight on what causes us to live without God's peace in our lives, and how we can reverse course and open our hearts to receive it. Also, Stanley gives his perspective on the things that hinder peace—including the "Four Great Hallmarks of God's Peace" and "Five Essential Beliefs for a Peaceful Heart"—to put the important message of this book into concrete terms. Addressing regret, anxiety, and fear, Dr. Stanley extends hope for overcoming the obstacles that block peace with the Lord. Finally, he gives direction on learning to live a life of contentment.

ISBN 0-7852-7297-6